ExO

Robin Liebe

ExtraOrdinary Leader
© 2009 Robin Liebe
Library of Congress Cataloging
Published by LuLu.com
Self-Improvement
ISBN 5-800028-582039
Printed in the Unites State of America

Contents:

ExO 1
Ordinary vs. Extraordinary

ExO 2
Unhealthy vs. Healthy

ExO 3
ExO Style

ExO 4
Team Building

ExO 5
Words from ExO Leaders

ExO 6
Healing

ExO 7
Focus

Introduction

At the end of the movie Castaway, starring Tom Hanks, he poured out his heart to his friend. He expressed that while he was stranded on the island in the Pacific Ocean for four years, he considered committing suicide. He made a rope out of tree bark, tied it around a chunk of tree that was tied to a branch on the side of the highest peak on the island. When he let it fall to test the branch, the branch broke. He said that for the first time he was in a place where he couldn't control anything. Those words rang in my ears. Have you ever felt like your grip on leadership just wasn't sustainable? Day in and day out, leaders are responsible for "controlling" things. They oversee the organization, employees, vision and the finances. It's a storm that seems to be unrehearsed, unpredictable, and unavoidable. But is that really true? Is it possible to see the storm coming and rehearse what you will do in it, predict how you'll handle it, and avoid the pitfalls that it brings?

To be an extraordinary leader, one must move beyond status quo leading. Being a status quo leader is going along with this fast-moving storm, getting caught up in its fury and then trying to clean up the devastation later. The problem with that is if unchecked, the dark side of the leader will come out. The dark side of a leader is when he leads for his own gain, without regard to his team. In recent times we've seen financial failure and jail time as people's actions, such as Bernie Madoff and others, have been discovered as illegal. The web was large and had destroyed hundreds of people's lives. What seemed to be forward progress in financial status and influence was nothing more than a shroud. Every leader has a dark side, and every leader has the option to either go with it, or resist it.

My goal for writing this book is to bring simplicity to your leadership. There are many options in deciding how to lead. Each of those options will bring a particular result. Unless you know what the options are and what the end result looks like, your leadership may resemble choosing straws. Leadership should not be guesswork. Once there is clarity, a specific plan can go forward and particular goals can be made and met, resulting in forward progress.

Being a status quo leader is not forward progress. When you're not going forward, you're either standing still or going backwards. A leader has the unique vantage point to help the people on his team find value and growth, not only within the realm of their occupation, but in their everyday life.

There is a way to lead that is extraordinary and not status quo. It takes a leader, looking in the mirror, willing to see the truth, instead of looking the mirror saying, "I'm okay. I like who I am and I don't need to change." Choosing to become an extraordinary leader does not require a Superman suit or a magic wand. Rather, it requires forward progress. To progress forward, the leader must desire to be a team player, with the hopes of being a motivator of growth and creativity for the team. This does not mean being a buddy. This simply means having genuine care and concern for the dreams, goals and visions of the team players.

Becoming an extraordinary leader takes time and a willingness to change. With those two components, you are well on your way to being an ExO (my term for extraordinary) leader. Because ExO leaders are hard to find, you may have never worked for, been mentored, or coached by an ExO leader. In writing this book, I am aware of that fact and have spent extra time in "explanation mode." An ExO leader is not a perfect leader, but a balanced leader. The key component of an ExO leader that you will soon come to realize is serving others. Now don't put this book down yet. You may have just had visions of Cinderella on her knees with a scrub brush in her hand, then translating that to you on your knees scrubbing the bathroom floors in your office in a suit and tie. This is not the image you should have.

Servant leadership is a style of leading that prefers others over yourself. This is just the tip of the iceberg, which is why becoming an ExO leader is a lifestyle change. It will make you a better spouse, friend, parent, and citizen. Being an extraordinary leader is freeing and it is fun! It allows you to be a part of the lives of those you work with. Their productivity goes up. Their creativity goes up. Your turn over is less. When people like to work for you, it will benefit you and your organization, whether you are a CEO, supervisor, pastor or a department head. It's a win-win situation. An extraordinary leader chooses to lead with positive influence rather than power. It is up to the leader to set the tone. Becoming an ExO leader is a road that's well worth walking on.

We will look at the leadership of people from the Bible, such as Jesus, David, Saul and Solomon, among others. The Bible has more to say than we have time to discover. I will attempt to present many thoughts to you, expecting that you will continue your study independently.

My hope is that throughout the pages of this book you will uncover new ways of leading that you can adapt to your life and leadership, as well as an encouragement to keep going in the right direction with a few extra tools. I desire for you, a leader with unlimited potential, to be willing to see where you've been status quo and begin the process of change. Leaders are all around us. They are teachers, company executives, pastors, department heads, coaches and so many more. When extraordinary leaders function at their best, the world is a better place.

The benefits to being an ExO leader are endless. Teams will function with freedom to reach the sky in their innovation. There are no limits to the team that an ExO leader builds up. Imagine you and your team waking up with excitement about your work and come in the doors ready to reach a little higher. It's possible. This is the role of an ExO leader; helping others see their potential and growing in it. It's a fun and rewarding role!

Before you make up your mind about which leader you are, begin at Chapter One. Start your journey to discover if you are an ordinary, status quo leader. Chapter six deals with how to heal if you've worked under an unhealthy leader, including some of my experiences.

Drawing from leaders in the Bible, you will learn some important ways to lead, as well as ways you might want to avoid. There's a lot to be said in between the beginning and the end! Enjoy your journey!

"You can judge your age by the amount of pain you feel when you come in contact with a new idea."

Pearl S. Buck

ExO 1
Ordinary vs. Extraordinary

In order to uncover what an extraordinary leader looks like, we must first talk about the ordinary way of leading. There are some leaders who don't want to rock the boat, and would like things to remain the same. This is a basic way to describe ordinary. Just go to work, do your normal duties and go back home – no extra effort required. Ordinary is the enemy of progress. Leadership is the very essence of progress and as a leader you should desire to go to the next level. Ordinary is small. Everyone is doing ordinary. Ordinary goes unnoticed most of the time because it doesn't stand out – it's mundane. It's so easy to go with the flow in a company or organization. Why bring added pressure with change when things are rolling along just fine? It's rolled like this for the past 20 years, and it'll continue to roll for another 20, right? Well, not really.

At some point, you, the leader, will need to recognize that ordinary will kill vision and will kill the dreams of those on the team around you. Ordinary breeds contempt. If leadership isn't willing to go beyond ordinary and take some risks, contempt will be bred into the team and will not stay hidden. At some point it will rise to the surface and the leader will be asked some questions such as, "Are you willing to go beyond ordinary leading to help this organization see a new level? If you're not willing to change to facilitate that, you may want to consider finding a new organization that is not requiring change." Harsh? No, just a reality that is necessary to observe in order for ordinary to move out of the way so you, the leader, can be an ExO leader and the organization can be extraordinary along with you.

Leaders should not be the only ones asking the tough questions, but also have the tough questions asked of them. Leaders are not untouchable. They may present themselves as that, but that is not reality. We are all accountable to someone, somewhere for how we lead and what we've done with the entrustment of our team and organization. Leadership is not a free for all. It's a gift that we must handle with care. We must take our passion for people, change and innovation, and lead others to new heights.

An ordinary organization is not innovative because the people on the team are not given a voice or goals with new heights to reach. *Their dreams do not have a voice.* The leader has the option to either lead his team with power, or lead them with influence. That is the line in the sand between ordinary and ExO. It is also the line between unhealthy and healthy, which we will spend the better part of this book discussing. So for now, ask yourself this question: What is more valuable to you – your position or the people on your team?

What is Extraordinary?

Being an ExO leader means doing things not too many leaders are doing. I am not referring to innovation. To be innovative refers to things, not people. To be extraordinary it takes having a vision and passion for the people on your team. Once you have that understanding and practice it, then innovation has a place to thrive.

ExO leaders do things for their team that no one else does. They notice, guide and mentor them. Why do so many leaders choose not to lead in an ExO way? Some may see it as hard work and don't want to take the time to change. Others may see it as a waste of time, choosing to stay on the status quo route because it's working just fine. An ExO leader deeply desires change. They aren't satisfied with status quo. They see the potential in the team around them. They see higher, broader and deeper than others. This may sound complex, but it's not. Case in point: Mother Theresa was an ExO leader because she loved. She saw higher than those who walked by the destitute and dying children on the curbs in India. She saw broader as she included others in her mission of love. She saw deeper as she built missions for these children to be well cared for. Mother Theresa was innovative, but her innovation came out of her ExO heart.

It takes heart to be an ExO leader. You cannot be a programmed and calloused leader and be ExO. You cannot care more about programs and yourself than you do your team. You cannot care more about the vertical aspect of the organization than you do the horizontal aspect. Vertical is where you see the company going. Horizontal are the people it takes to get it there. They are the ones who work on your left and your right every day. If you care about their involvement in the organization, as well as their teaching and training, you are well on your way to being an ExO leader.

Being an ExO leader will require some action from you. You will need to evaluate your leadership style. There are many styles of leadership. Everyone who has a leadership gifting can attain the highest level available to them through two basic principles: Humility and servant hood. Rarely do we hear or see the words, "humility and servant hood" in the same context as the word "leader." You can read about being an ExO leader, but if you don't have humility and a heart to serve those on your team, all the conferences you've attended and all the books you've read won't be of much value to you.

Leaders are a multi-faceted group of people. A leader tends to be a motivator. They see things that need to change or be improved. The goal is to learn how to apply that personally as well as training others in what they have tried and learned. Sometimes problems arise when a leader follows the belief that he must gain as much power as possible, which places him in a position of control. This is a danger for any leader. *Being a leader is not a rise to power, but a rise of influence. With influence comes a voice that can only be heard through relationship, humility and respect.* Strength as a leader is humility and the trust that comes with it. If the goal of a leader is to control as much as possible he will be sorely disappointed when there is nothing left to control. He will be left with a long, hard fall to the bottom of the ladder he worked so hard to climb, even to the point of stepping on others to get there. Leadership should not be about the rungs in a ladder. It's about the journey to become a leader who serves with a positive influence and considers the whole team.

When we hear the word "leadership" it's easy to identify it with someone who sits alone behind a mahogany desk in a black leather chair, in a big corner office, making decisions all by themselves. The culture today is backing away from that model of leadership as it has oftentimes bred rebellion towards the leader. It leaves no room for others to be a vital part of a team. In actuality, that type of leading is the hardest as it leaves no room for error on the part of the leader. If an incorrect decision is made, he is at fault. He didn't have a team around him to help make the decision. Still there are leaders who have a team but do not utilize them in a healthy way. They use their authority to trump the thoughts and concerns of the team, doing it their own way regardless of what the team feels.

Leadership is a gift and a tool given to us for a specific purpose. Leading others to greatness can be one of the most fulfilling gifts. Healthy leadership can also be the most rewarding as you lead those around you to heights they thought were unattainable. In order for that to happen, the foundation needs to be healthy. If a foundation is not built from health, it will not have healthy attributes and it will crumble.

The world is full of leaders - young leaders and seasoned ones. Oftentimes a leader's thoughts tends to be for the purpose of making his life better, but leaders also have a major role in the development of other leaders. The leadership gift just keeps on giving!

There are many aspects to leading the healthy way,

which we will explore and discover throughout the pages of this book. No matter what name or title a leader is given, whether boss, supervisor, manager, pastor or CEO, he is either healthy or unhealthy. That is what sets an ordinary leader apart from an ExO leader. Let's describe what those roles are.

"You do not lead by hitting people over the head – that's assault, not leadership."

Dwight D. Eisenhower

ExO 2
Unhealthy vs. Healthy

The Unhealthy Leader:

No one wants to be described as unhealthy. We need to take an honest look at what an unhealthy leader is in order to discover what a healthy leader looks like. An unhealthy leader is one who seems to know "everything" and tries to convince others of his knowledge. He chooses not to learn from those around him, making him ordinary in most every way. This leader is living in the past, taking what he's always known, choosing not to implement much from today's teaching. He already has his mind made up. This leader is afraid of change, but won't readily admit it. He'd rather keep doing what he's always done because it's the most comfortable. His philosophy keeps him from changing. He thinks he is a team leader, but his definition of team is that those around him support only him and his ideas. He expects everyone under his authority to do as he says. If they don't, they risk the ridicule of not supporting him as the leader and ultimately risk losing their job. Their voice is not welcomed as the leader's voice is supposed to be the loudest. His idea of a "win" for his team is when they all agree with everything he believes and says, as well as obey his every command without asking any questions. The lack of relationship keeps him in this high place, not allowing the voices to be heard from where he sits. This leader revels in power – power over others and the control it brings. This leader is not in it for the team, but strictly for himself. One thing that marks an unhealthy leader is when those around him, meaning those who are under his authority, fear him. When he walks into the room and people become unresponsive, this could be one indication of an unhealthy leader. When leaders realize that people will do more for them out of respect than out of fear, much more will be accomplished.

The Ladder: A Team of One

The best way I have found to describe this leader in visual terms is this: Visualize a ladder. The first thing to notice is the position the ladder is in. It's vertical. It goes up high, but allowing only one person to go higher. The unhealthy leader sees an opportunity for success and begins to climb this ladder rung by rung. Who do you think is going to stabilize this leader's success? It's those who are on the team. Instead of being allowed to let their innovation thrive, they are busy holding up the ladder of success for this one leader. Their hands are being controlled and their minds burdened.

Their hands are not idol, but they are bound in making sure this leader is being lifted to new heights. Their minds are being strained with the messages this leader sends down to them. The demands keep coming down to the team from this leader, straining them with his desired success. *The ladder represents a team of one.* Relationships are not being built between this leader and his team. What he may see as a bond with his team is merely his desire to go higher as they clutch the ladder. They are bonded to his demands, but not to his vision. He cares more about positional authority than influence. Simply put, because he's the boss they are required to obey. The "ladder leader" cannot be flexible or he will fall off the perch he's created for himself. His leading techniques are rigid and harsh. This leader gets frustrated easily and often.

One thing this unhealthy, demanding leader doesn't notice is that his fate is in the hands of this team. They have the availability to release his ladder at any moment, and eventually do. They get to a point where they are taxed, stressed and ready to move on, putting this leader in an unstable place, which allows for his ladder to fall. In other words, the team gets tired of holding this leader up. They get tired of the demands to help him get higher and they eventually burn out and let go.

The Healthy Leader:

The healthy leader chooses to learn about leadership. He takes what he already knows and builds his life on that, adding new teaching on a regular basis. This leader welcomes new revelation and implements it in accordance with what he's already learned in the past. He is not afraid of change. In fact, he welcomes it with open arms. His idea of team leadership is to hear what others are saying, He wants them to support the goal, of whatever sort it is.

The healthy leader remains within reach of the team, in order to keep them as vital assets to the team. He makes sure they feel that the team cannot win without them and their ideas. He willingly sets his personal agenda aside in order to make sure the entire team is going in the same direction, even if he feels there is a diversion from his original plan. The leader must guide the team in the right direction, but taking into account their passions and the goals they see for the organization. This leader leads out of integrity. A healthy leader knows how to express himself with openness and honesty and teach others to do the same.

The mark of a healthy leader is when his employees, or those under his authority, are not afraid of him. People should be at peace when spending time around you. Health + Openness = The ExO leader. Notice I did not say the perfect leader; there is no such person. We all have health issues to work through. To become healthy in areas where we are not, will take openness on our part.

The Horizon: A Team of Many

The healthy leader does not climb a ladder. Instead, he leads horizontally. When you look at the horizon, your sight goes from side to side. Leading horizontally is the same way. It takes a leader who knows how to look left and right at the team around him, but also how to lead them higher. To be a healthy leader takes a horizontal style with a vertical goal. This simply means that you see success as the whole team having a voice and everyone having a place of success. The healthy leader knows how to link arms and opinions, and successfully move them forward. That does not mean that everyone takes a step forward at the same time. It does mean leaving room for those who are a step behind and a step ahead. As long as there is forward motion, goals can be reached. Horizontal leadership also means that this leader can see when it's time to stop and discuss the vision. That can't be done if the leader is up on a ladder all by himself. He can break from the team line up to step out in front and walk horizontally, side to side, looking people in the eye and leading them to the goal. This leader is visually available and willing to listen to his team.

There is a well-written children's story that has significant truths for leaders. It is the story of a leader named Yertle the Turtle by Dr. Seuss. The setting is in a pond, of which Yertle is the king. One day he realizes he can't see enough. He demands that turtles begin to stack up under him so he can see farther. His belief was that if he could see it, he was the king of it. His demands grew larger, as he got tired of the same scene and realized there was more to be king of. He demanded more turtles to stack up, that is, until the stack was so pressurized that the guy on the bottom burped and brought the whole bunch down, including this selfish king. I encourage you to read the story in its entirety. There are a few things you can learn from this child's story that could help you discover if you are a healthy or unhealthy leader.

How Do You See It?

The scene in the beginning of this child's story

might be what you see in your life. Life is good. Everyone is working in his proper "corner". The boss is happy, the coffee is hot, and nothing can go wrong. Everyone is working in sync. The money is good. Everyone is satisfied. It's like a well-oiled machine. It's running good, smooth and without issues. We like it that way. It's a perfect environment for innovative people to dream the next biggest way of living. It's the best way to allow people to be the most productive. Yes, everyone is quite happy in deed!

But, oh how quickly the peace evaporates. As a leader, you are responsible for the peace of the office. If not kept in check, or held accountable, it's very easy to slip into the demanding mode. All of a sudden, this leader seems to think he deserves more. His current position isn't enough for him. He goes from being the "boss" to being just plain "bossy."

This unhealthy leader suddenly feels *entitled* to more. He makes his position into a position it was never meant to be. This leader becomes demanding based on his self-given right to be more than his title gives adherence to. Simply put, he becomes selfish. When a leader becomes selfish, things get ugly in a hurry. All of a sudden, this leader thinks something is wrong in his position. He becomes unsatisfied with his current position and sadly, he may even be in the top position, which gives him the authority, whether right, wrong, or indifferent, to begin to demand of those in positions below his.

Selfishness keeps a leader from seeing the truth. It lies to you and says you need more to be satisfied. If you believe this lie, as a leader you become restless with your position and begin wanting more. You will want to go higher. The sad thing is that many other people could be in your position, but they aren't – you are. Leaders have a choice to lead out of selfishness and work the company's budget, schedule, and perks to benefit them the most, or they can lead out of a team mentality and make sure their team is being cared for as well. I am not suggesting a "spread the wealth" way of leading. I am suggesting a "spread the respect" way of leading. It's okay for the "top dog" to make more money than others, but it isn't okay for the "top dog" to use that money to manipulate others and seek out personal gain putting the company or organization in jeopardy.

Leaders may have perks, but with it comes great responsibility.

There is one factor that must remain as leaders gain influence, and that is humility.

Unhealthy leaders take their humility and toss it to the way side and chose to listen to the selfish voices instead. The selfish voices tell you that you deserve to be in charge of more. They tell you that you have a right to more, a right to be the boss of more people and the right to do and say whatever you want simply because you're the "king" of all you see.

This leader becomes selfish, demanding and greedy. He allows that selfishness to rule his actions, which paves the way for him to rule with a heavy hand. We all face this potential. It begins with little things such as a reimbursement that you turn is as a business transaction, but you know it really wasn't. You end up doing "little" things that are tainted, but they end up being big things that will take you and the organization down. This is not an unusual activity. It happens every day around the world. America has seen some substantial cases of selfish money moguls and political figures.

Take for instance the situation with Bernie Madoff. On March 12, 2009 he went to jail for the first time based on his theft of $65 billion by falsely investing other people's money. He started out as a lifeguard and lawn sprinkler installer. In 1960 he founded his company, Madoff Investment Securities Llc, using $5,000 from his savings he earned from his previous two occupations. As time went on, his gift of management turned heads at Wall Street, feeding this aggressive beast that was rising up inside of Bernie. This major money making job allowed Bernie and his family to live a lifestyle most only dream of. Wealth is not the problem. The problem is the dark, selfish side each of us has which includes a deep desire for power. When money is involved, people will be ripped off every time. This need for power and being in charge is a prison all of it's own. When people are caught, their prison bars are just a manifestation of how they've been leading all along – from their own prison of selfishness.

On January 30, 2009 Gov. Blagoiavich (IL) was impeached from his office as Governor from federal corruption charges that included attempting to sell President Barak Obama's U.S. Senate seat. As the Chicago Tribune said, the Illinois Senate "ousted one governor for abusing his power and anointed another who built his political career around having no power at all." The lieutenant governor, Patrick Quinn, was sworn in as

Governor just hours after the impeachment. How did this happen? The same dark side that took Bernie to prison: selfishness. From the same article in the Chicago Tribune, written by Ray Long and Rick Pearson, these words were penned: "But that was enough for lawmakers, who had long pondered impeaching a governor they assailed as arrogant and untrustworthy. All the while, federal agents were investigating his administration for acts of wrongdoing involving hiring, contracting, board appointments and fundraising." New Illinois Governor Patrick Quinn also makes this statement referring to changes he would make: "…he would take down costly specially made signs with Blagojevich's name from I-PASS collection lanes on the Illinois Tollway. Quinn said he would not replace them with his own." Quinn also said, "I am not for this imperial governorship routine."

That's the difference between healthy and unhealthy – status quo and ExO. One is arrogant and one is humble. One wants power and one wants to empower others.

Madoff and Blagoiavich had influence and power at their fingertips. Somewhere those "little" things turned into big things, which brought Federal Agents to their doors. They led with selfishness, using the perks to feed the hungry beast of pride, causing their own demise. They are not alone. You and I have the same appetite inside of us. Some are just better at starving it than others.

It is easy for leaders to become arrogant and prideful. Pride says, "I can do this on my own!" This is self-sufficiency, showing this leader needs to be a follower before he can be a leader. When one leads out of self-sufficiency, he will put his eagerness to lead ahead of his ability to lead, resulting in failure.

1 Peter 5:2-3 will help us in this matter. Here we read very clearly the kind of leader God wants us to be. Verses 2-3 (MSG) say this: "…that you care for God's flock with all the diligence of a shepherd. Not because you have to, but because you want to please God. Not calculating what you can get out of it, but acting spontaneously. Not bossily telling others what to do, but tenderly showing the way."

Are you banking on your title as a way of receiving respect? That is calculating what you can get out of it. That is where a line is crossed and instead of being a shepherd who is gentle and leads out of relationship, you will lead out of authority, causing fear in those under and around you.

Leading out of Relationship vs. Leading out of Authority

As a leader, you have a responsibility for the teaching and training of those around you, but sometimes that can be taken to an unhealthy level. In order to be an effective ExO leader, it takes respect and relationship. Without that, the leader becomes a stumbling block to the team. To have influence means you have to be close to those you lead. It supports the intimate way of leading, which simply means letting them into your life.

Authoritative

An authoritative leader leads with control and he seems very cold to his team. It is at this point that the leader begins to place unrealistic demands on others who are under his authority. This is of no benefit to them, thus taking out the relationship factor. It becomes an, I say, "jump" and you say "how high," type of leadership. This type of authoritative leading leaves no room for other leaders to express themselves. Their identity is covered and kept silent so as to keep the spotlight on one leader only. No one else is allowed to share in the success, as though they didn't have a part in the forming of it.

This leader will set himself up in what he thinks is a higher position of authority, giving him a better perspective on his "kingship". When a leader moves into this type of mindset, he will begin to place *unrealistic demands* on others. His perspective changes to a "me" mentality instead of a team leadership style. He wants those under his authority to support him and his goals. The pressure from this style of leadership will eventually cause major fallout, as we will talk about later.

The people this leader demands of, will do what they are asked to do. They are obeying reluctantly and with a strained relationship. He has moved himself into positional authority where he is not accountable to anyone. He is not looking for relationship. He only wants obedience. The bottom line is, he requires it, not accepting anything less. This starts an unhealthy pattern of stress to build up in the rest of the staff. They no longer have a voice. He doesn't want to hear what they have to say because he is the "king" and their job is to listen and obey.

When the team decides to obey and not fight this type of leader, he seems happy for a while. But in time, he will become unsatisfied again and begin demanding more from the team. When this happens, the voices in the team will still be silenced, building up more pressure inside them. In time the leader becomes unsatisfied. He is very sensitive to what the staff under him says and does, much like having a microscope on them. They can't do much that is right. He can tell they aren't totally supporting him.

This leader creates a lot of stress on those under him. All he wants is their full participation, without any questions asked. The team just wants to work without that kind of pressure. They are loyal and obedient, but under this kind of stress, that can only last a short time, as we will see later.

In the case of Bernie Madoff, his sons Mark and Andrew, who held trading positions at Bernard L Madoff Investment Securities, insisted they "had no knowledge whatsoever of the fraud". The two were responsible for blowing the whistle on their father after he told them: "It's all just one big lie." (telegraph.co.uk) Somewhere, something snapped. Just as in the Madoff family, there will come a time in other corporations when someone in the group will be brave enough to voice their stress and their concern, hoping to be heard. They just want to be validated and cared for, so they risk it by speaking up. This may or may not go well because of the stress and the strain that is building up. They feel this is their only hope, since their leader isn't noticing what he's doing to them.

Being a brave voice in the crowd is risky business.

You may be heard, validated and appreciated. But then again you may not. This unhealthy leader doesn't like being told about negative issues because it's a reflection on him, implying that he isn't a good leader. *He is going deeper and deeper into denial, blinded from seeing what's really going on in the team below him.*

Leaders in this stage will often feel that it's their job and within the boundaries of their authority to put the people under them through the "press." Since they've had to go through it, so do you. They often feel it's their job to help you be a martyr, but they describe it as being taught to be a servant.

The problem with this type of leadership is they become demanding. They cross over the boundaries of healthy leadership and move into an unhealthy, even abusive place. These types of leaders hurt a lot of people, but they seem to see it as helping you understand pain, because as a leader, you should understand what pain is, and they are here to help you learn the hard way. When leaders rule with an iron fist, they are afraid of losing control, causing them to lead through dominance. But as a Christian leader, we should know that the Holy Spirit is an influencer. He is not demanding or controlling. It requires taking care of God's flock "with all the diligence of a shepherd." That just means to take extra effort and persistence to make sure you've done it right. When it's not being done right, you will just be "bossily telling others what to do." Then coaching turns into criticism really fast.

Coaching vs. Criticism

Coaching requires relationship, or all that is left is criticism. There is a grand difference between the two. Coaching is based on verbal encouragement, and criticism is based on verbal discouragement. One builds up and one tears down. It takes a healthy leader to know how to coach. If you've ever been on a sports team, you know there are coaches who are healthy in their leadership, and those who aren't. Yelling and screaming is not coaching, it's just being loud. Just because you're loud doesn't mean people hear you. They may fear you, but they don't hear you. Coaching includes constructive criticism, or encouragement to do things a new or different way without putting a person down, or demeaning him in any way.

Portrait of a Coach

A coach is someone who mentors another person, with specific goals in mind. A coach is a motivator, encourager and a friend. A coach can be the leader who is in authority, but not be authoritative. There is a difference between a coach who humbly leads another person to reach specific goals, and a coach who is authoritative and makes the goals for someone. There are a three things it takes to be a healthy coach.

1. Humility
Leaders who are humble are allowed through doors that prideful leaders are not. The key word is "allowed." Prideful leaders force themselves through doors that were never open to them. Humble leaders don't do that. Instead, they quietly offer their life to others and not just an opinion. They genuinely care about the person they are coaching. This investment is purely out of humility, offering

whatever they can to assist someone else.

2. Respect

I have seen leaders who enter into coaching relationships but do not respect those they are speaking into. Their relationship is based on the coach doing all the talking and the "student" receiving a lecture on life. This is not the least bit respectful. Listening is one of the most respectful attributes a coach can have. He may have a lot of wisdom to share, but if he cannot be a listener and respect the other person, his wisdom will not be welcomed or received. As a coach, you have to earn the right to be heard. Your title isn't going to earn you that right. Humility and respect will. If someone opens up their life to you, be honored and treat it carefully. Sometimes they just need to talk about life. Other times they will need thoughtful guidance, or a gentle warning. If given with respect, people can receive most anything you say. Mix humility with respect and you will have a strong coaching relationship.

3. Relationship

This brings us to the third way to be a healthy coach. Too often, the coaching relationship tends to be the coach talking and the other person listening. If this is the case, not only is the coach not humble or respectful, but there is not going to be a chance for a relationship. Sometimes leaders have the belief that in order to coach someone they need to remain in their place of authority. The chance of a true coaching relationship happening is very slim under these conditions. Not only that, but sometimes leaders who are authoritative don't desire a relationship, falsely believing that if they become friends, their voice is somehow less significant. Because of this, relationship cannot be built up and the coach will not be heard or respected. In addition, relationship takes time. Be patient with whom you're coaching. Let life happen and relationship will evolve out of it. What's the rush? Keep conversations as simple and stream lined as possible. Here's how that looks: When coaching someone, they may just need someone to bring clarity to their life and simplify their thoughts and goals. When someone has a myriad of thoughts, dreams and beliefs, it generally takes a while to unpack all of that and bring it all into perspective. To do this it will take humility, respect and relationship. It can be done. I know from experience that these points actually work. Leading in this manner is fun and it allows for the one being coached to participate in his life change, releasing the coach from bearing the weight of it.

    When a leader is healthy, his desire is to teach people what he knows for the sake of benefiting that person, not to bring out peacock feathers for people to say, "Wow! You're magnificent!" Some of the best coaches are faceless. Some are even nameless. Greatness in leadership should not be to have your name known. An ExO leader doesn't desire fame, but to pass on what he knows in order to benefit the world one person at a time. To do this, it takes relationship, not power. A relational leader looks for potential in others. When a leader spends his time looking for the bad in people instead of the good, he's anti-team and non-productive. It's a vicious circle. The leader wants results, but is then frustrated when the result he wants doesn't come because he's either not looking for them, or has not coached his team in how to give those results. Do you lead out of relationship or out of authority?

In order to be an ExO leader, you must ask yourself these questions: What condition is your team in? Are they excited to be on your team, or are they distant and waiting for the next "put down" session, I mean the next staff meeting? Criticism is deadly. It tears at a person's very being. An organization cannot grow in a poisonous environment. People will leave your team and find one that is healthy, uplifting and beneficial to their career and personal life.

An ExO leader thinks not only of what he says, but also how he says it. Will the meeting you have with your staff members help them, encourage them, or make them want to quit? What condition will they go home in after being in your company today? Is your leadership benefiting their life, or are you attempting to control their life? Tough questions. An ExO leader is stable enough to ask and answer these types of questions honestly. Do you want to be a coach that builds a team, or are you a critical leader who is anti-team?

The Fear Factor

When a leader functions in an unhealthy, authoritative manner, the team around him begins to fear him. Proverbs 1:7 says, "The fear of the Lord is the beginning of knowledge; fools despise wisdom and instruction." (NASB) If you are a leader who causes others to fear you, you have moved into a prideful way of leading and have placed yourself in the seat that only God is deserving of. We are to point people to the fear of God (which is reverent and holy), rather than making them afraid of us.

One thing an unhealthy leader who leads with fear deals with is territorialism, or the belief that all he sees, he owns. I will describe this in greater detail toward the end of the book. Simply put, that just means that this leader has a need to be popular and have a high approval rating. He doesn't want to hear what's wrong. He's higher on his ladder than ever before and is beginning to distance himself from reality. He will react to anyone who speaks against his authority. In his strong reaction he will remind the lone, brave voice just who he really is. He's the king, and don't forget it. He continues this pattern by becoming sharp and closed-minded. He doesn't want to be questioned. Instead, he once again defines where his authority really lies, and it seems to be everywhere. He now extends his authority to a higher place, which will now require more support from the staff or the employees. But the problem is, his support is diminishing. He is obviously not the kind of leader who will simply ask for people to support his vision, but instead he demands it. The brave voices don't really have a choice, since this boss is the king and you don't say "no" to a king.

By now, the unhealthy leader has so far removed himself from reality he can't see how brash and rough he has become. He sees only one thing, and that is his vision of all the things he wants that are far off, expecting everyone else to make it happen, no matter what.

This type of leadership doesn't affect just a few staff members. *In time, it will affect entire families.* The fear will spread and affect more than this leader realizes. They won't tell him because they are afraid of him. They know he will find out how they feel anyway and level a charge at them without it being based on reality, increasing their desire to be distanced from him. As the other staff members obey out of fear, they climb over that brave voice, increasing his pressure. His load just got heavier as the other staff members lift this "king" up so he can see more, be in charge of more and feel like he has the full support of his office staff.

What happens at this point is this leader perches up high on his throne celebrating his success, but it's going to cost him. He doesn't know that yet. When you're in a high place, celebrating your success, it will not only get lonely, but you will soon become dissatisfied. This place of rulership won't last forever because the foundation is shaky and unstable. The brave staff members who have been demanded of for support can't sustain the pressure forever. There will come a time of shaking and breaking.

Usually a leader like this thinks that the problem with the team lies within that one who spoke up, trying to alert him to the fact that his team cannot live under this type of pressure very long. Now why pick on this guy? Here's why: Because this quiet, steady voice is a leader too. The other staff members follow him. The boss picked this person on purpose. If the boss can control him, then he can control the entire staff. The use of intimidation seems to work for this type of leader, as it causes fear. If you are a leader who likes to intimidate others, then there are some deeper issues in your life you should take a look at. This is obviously a very unhealthy leadership style, yet this happens everyday in many occupations.

There's no way this brave staff member will be able to sustain this kind of pressure. In desperation, he will once again take a risk to voice his opinion, already knowing what the boss will say, but hoping that he has somehow changed. This staff member really doesn't want to complain. He's never been a complainer before, but is now placed in a situation where he has to say something. The other staff members are depending on it. He feels the pressure to be the change agent. He speaks for the whole group. It's not just this lone employee feeling the stress and strain anymore; it's now felt by all the others in this situation.

When a leader puts himself in the place of pretending to be "king," it becomes impossible for him to see who this lone voice really is. This lone voice gets treated as someone he is not, and ends up being distanced from this demanding leader. The leader doesn't see that, since he sees only his vision, not the vision as a whole. What he does see is what he views as rebellion. Even though this lone employee has been a good employee, having been submissive and obedient, his boss now treats him as rebellious. But that's not reality. This unhealthy boss is the one who's moved into pride and has distanced himself from the truth. The employee, or staff member is being treated as someone he is not. This breeds intense amounts of frustration on him, since he knows that his boss once knew who he was but has since gone further down the road of bad leadership.

The strain between these two has reached a height that the boss is not able to see. He seems to think that if he can get high enough in his leadership, he'll be able to conquer everything. Why does he desire that? So he can control it. Somewhere pride and arrogance slipped in. The Bible says that "pride goes before a fall," (Proverbs 16:18

NIV). This unhealthy boss is too busy looking for more things to conquer and control that he seems to have forgotten that truth.

The employee desperately tries to get his boss's attention. He acknowledges what the boss is seeing, but reminds him that it's not all about him. There are others in the office that have a voice, dreams and goals.

That is a sad day. Everyone has been given a passion for something, and when you are on the job, carrying a particular passion, it is the leaders job to help make that passion a reality through coaching. If as a leader you are unhealthy, you will never see what the passion is in those under your leadership. You would be too wrapped up in making sure the staff under you is making *your* passion become reality.

It is at this point that this lone voice, this employee who is desperate to be heard, comes to a breaking point. *This is called burnout.* When a boss or a leader continually asks an employee, or people on his team to bend their morals or to support something they do not agree with or believe in, they burnout.

There are four levels of burnout, climaxing at a point when one is prescribed medication and must receive counseling because the pressure has caused them to "crack". *People cannot withstand the pressure this type of leader puts them under for a sustained amount of time.* The reason for burnout is there are continuing circumstances that are forced on them outside of their control, causing them to be pushed to a breaking point. They are unable to change the circumstances, unless they quit their job and go elsewhere. That is easier said than done, as they have built up retirement or have great insurance.

There comes a time when this employee, who is loyal to the company, will speak up for everyone and continue to plead with his boss, begging him to see their need. They want to be well tended to. *They just want to be noticed, cared for and validated.* An unhealthy boss has his head in the clouds making him unable to notice and has become unwilling to listen to a subordinate.

When the leadership continues in this path, those under his leadership get starved. If it's spiritual leadership behaving in this manner, the starvation includes spirituality. Encompassed in this is also a starvation of love, acceptance, vision and guidance. Without those components in a leader, there is broken trust, suspicion, anger and frustration. It's not only the one lone voice who starves in this situation, but all the other employees placed under this leader. This would include a congregation, a company or an administration. When people are starving, they don't have energy. They become lethargic and wander around without vision or purpose, pushing them further and further into a burnout mode. This unhealthy leader will be held accountable. Leaders like this have removed themselves from accountability, but will one day fall from the very thing they've built up.

One would think that at some point this leader would see the truth and change his ways, but he is stubborn, arrogant and determined to get his way because he sees only one thing, and that is the very thing that will benefit *him* the most. He won't let anyone take it away from him. If he feels that you, or anyone else is threatening that, he bites back hard. This type of leader will most often choose to fire those on his team who speak up and speak out against him. He has become insecure and feels that this one individual does not support him and his self-centered goals. He also believes his staff member is spreading his beliefs to everyone else on the staff. This leader still cannot see the truth because he is so far removed from it as he functions in denial.

Before he fires that one lone voice, reminding him of his authority by saying, "I'm the boss around here." This not only silences him, but it reveals how this leader is threatened by any questions that would not only bring clarity and accountability, of which he has far removed himself from because he feels he has risen to a place where he has to answer to no one.

Using the "me centered" model of leadership is destructive. The tower of Babel (Genesis 11:1-9) was built on the same premise of "I rule from the clouds." When a leader who functions in this style believes that nothing can be higher than me...not a lawyer, not a board or it's members, not a company bylaw...no, nothing," then watch out, you're about to have a very, very long fall. And when you crash down from your tower, things will be shaken right out of you.

Pride vs. Humility

Pride weaves itself into ones life through several different means. The outstanding way is through preying on our basic need for approval, value and importance.

Pride is the act of trying to be like God: all knowing, all sufficient and sovereign. Pride is a sin, but yet all of us have been born into it and spend a lifetime trying to rid ourselves of it. When we aren't ridding ourselves of it, we are cooperating with it. Pride says I'm entitled to more: more authority, more money, etc. This is the "me" centered way to live and lead. Leaders who are prideful are blinded to their over-sized ego problem. When alerted by those around them, chances are they will fail to see it, resulting in their long, hard fall. This is disheartening because this leader probably has excellent leadership skills buried somewhere within him. But when allowed, pride will blind one from seeing how to accurately use this talent, such as in the case of King Saul.

Saul and David

You may recall the story of King Saul found in the book of 1 Samuel 8 -31. Saul was in a powerful position. In time, he allowed this power to rule him. Pride edged its way into his life and opened the door for jealously, disobedience, and other sins to thrive.

Saul was a powerful leader. He was given David, the shepherd boy, as a gift. God took His spirit from Saul and gave him a distressing one instead. Because of this, his servants suggested someone to be invited to play the harp for him. It so happened that David, the shepherd boy, was skillful with the harp. He was beckoned from the pasture to attend to Saul. Whenever this distressing spirit tormented Saul, David played and the spirit left him, making David a gift to Saul.

David was also anointed to be the next king after Saul. He was faithfully sitting in his future palace, playing his harp for the king he was going to replace. Think about that for a minute. Imagine you are David. How would you have felt? What would you have done? It would have been very easy for David to allow his heart to become prideful. But in his humility, he kept quiet and faithfully did what he was invited to do.

If Saul would have been a healthy leader, he would have been secure in his position and would have mentored David, also knowing David was a man of valor, a man of war, a great orator and handsome to top it off. But Saul did something many leaders do: he became threatened, turned to anger that eventually led to resentment. Saul was not going to let David be more powerful than him. The thing is, David couldn't be more powerful than Saul. He was a shepherd boy. But he was an anointed shepherd boy who was humble and willing to wait for his turn to be king. If Saul would have realized that David was not going to rush the throne and steal the crown from him, maybe he wouldn't have become so jealous. But reality is, Saul didn't resist his dark side and it ate at him, causing him to do many foolish things. It was Saul's own behavior that caused the undoing of his throne. In the end, it caused him and his son to be killed and their dead bodies put on display.

John Maxwell, in The Maxwell Leadership Bible, describes the difference between Saul and David's way of leading, from 1 Samuel 24:1-22. He describes Saul as:

1. Self-conscience from the beginning.
2. Presumed on the priestly office.

3. Disobeyed God in the little things.
4. Lost integrity by covering his sin.
5. Failed to submit to God-given authority.
6. Preoccupied with his own fame.

He also describes David as:
1. Displayed God-confidence.
2. Didn't assume any right or privilege.
3. Obeyed God in the little things.
4. Maintained integrity by respecting Saul.
5. Consistently submitted to authority.
6. Desired to increase God's reputation.

One was full of pride and the other, humility. It isn't hard to tell who was prideful and who wasn't. David respected King Saul, even while Saul threw spears at him. When Saul and his company were tracking David down to kill him, David had the chance to kill Saul, but his humility and respect for God's authority held him back. David knew how to come under authority. He knew Saul was anointed by God for that role and he wasn't going to cross the line of authority. David could have easily become prideful when he was anointed to be king. He also could have become prideful when invited to play his harp for King Saul. But David understood that God is the one who anointed him for a later time. Think of it. David was out tending sheep in the pasture, probably playing on his harp and writing a Psalm, hymn or song. He was called home to have a prophet anoint him to be king, then he returned to the pasture to continue tending the sheep and playing the harp. David was not wrapped up in titles. I am sure he was humbled and honored at what lay ahead in his future. Even so, he continued to spend his time serving his father and his God. I can imagine his song writing flourished after that! God was his focus. That is what makes him one of the most amazing leaders in history. Even when he could have become prideful, he didn't. He could have allowed his kingly anointing to cause him to forget his Godly focus and instead focus on what he'd look like in a crown. Is that what happens when you get a promotion? Does your heart change? It takes a lot of work to stay focused on humility when promotion comes. If you keep God as your focus, you won't get side tracked and fall into pride. Keep playing your harp and keep writing Psalms, hymns and songs. Why stop? The higher up you go, the more you're going to need those Psalms, hymns and songs! If you are passionate about God instead of power, promotion will cause you to worship Him and you won't allow others to worship you.

While Israel was at war with the Philistines, David had two jobs. He was Saul's armor bearer, as well as still returning back home to tend to his aging father's sheep! Now he has been promoted as the king's armor bearer, but is still herding sheep. It is obvious to see David's faithfulness, but also his humility. Anointed to be king, but carrying the current king's armor around *and* tending his father's sheep. This is truly astounding.

Even still, while returning back to the war with the Philistines, David had heard enough from Goliath and went out to fight him. Remember, this is in front of the Israelite army *and* the king. This young shepherd, anointed to be king and without armor, walked out in front of a champion fighter and stood his ground. With one stone in his sling, he called on God to make it hit the target. Goliath died that day. David, the king's armor bearer, who was anointed to be the next king, dealt with his country's enemy that day, in humility. He did not act out of pride or a title. David's identity was secure in God.

Because of this victory, Saul saw something in David and put him in charge of the Israelite army. David quickly by-passed all the ranks and went straight to the top. This was not because he was seeking it. Because of his humility, God exalted him to a higher position. The people gave David more praise than their king. They praised David for killing tens of thousands and praised Saul for killing his thousands. David could have used this popular opinion to overthrow Saul, but he didn't. Look at this for a moment. As a leader, if you become jealous when someone on your team has what you may feel is more success than you, then your team of one is in a dangerous place. This was not a good day for Saul. Somewhere within Saul was a jealousy and an insecurity that he was not about to run from. Instead, he ran to it, causing his pride to have a place in his life. It didn't take long and Saul treated David like an enemy. That is because he truly believed David wanted his throne. Saul became suspicious of David and began to make decisions to do all that he could to control David.

Let's examine that for a moment. David is already anointed to take the throne, and he is willing to humbly wait for it. But Saul, who is already the king, is convinced that David's kindness and humility are really a ploy to dethrone him and take over. Saul became suspicious and it drove him insane. He was chasing something that wasn't really there. Inviting David into the palace was not a blank check. Saul had strings attached. He wanted to control David, but Saul's pride deceived him into believing that David's gracious behavior was really devious. As it happened to be, David and Saul's son, Jonathan, become best friends, which also caused jealousy in Saul. Saul never moved past his deception, crippling his own leadership. That is the travesty of it all. There are amazing leaders who have trapped themselves because of pride.

Saul allowed his anger and suspicion to rule him so much that twice he threw a spear at David, but David escaped. The root of this behavior was fear: fear that David was more loved than he was and fear that David would steal the throne from him. Saul knew God was with David and had allowed Saul to be tormented. So Saul sent David out of his sight and put him over his army. This was not just an out-of-sight, out-of-mind decision. He could clearly see God's hand was on David. The healthy thing to do would have been to use the occasion to train David in kingly ways. He could have blessed David as his successor. But leaders who are in this state are unable to bless those who come after them. When an unhealthy leader, such as Saul, is more wrapped up in fighting for his authority, he won't allow anyone else to have it. When a leader attempts to own authority, it will most definitely be painfully ripped from him. I have this saying I repeat to myself often: "I own nothing." If we can allow that to become a foundation of all our thoughts, health is sure to follow. If Saul had lived that, he would have spared himself much grief. But because he clung tightly to his title, position and authority, he missed life-enhancing opportunities to mentor David and bless his reign. This is very sad because it still happens today. Far too many leaders allow their title and position to become their identity. Toward the end of my book I will talk further on the matter of identity. For now I will say that if your identity is not found in Christ, this will be your undoing. It is remarkable that even though Saul didn't bless David, David blessed Saul. Matthew 5:44 says to love your enemies and pray for those who persecute you. Do you have a Saul in your life? Many of us have at one time or another. Are you showing him love? Are you blessing him, even if it's not being returned?

Unhealthy leaders who are full of jealousy and insecurity do strange things. You might feel persecuted from the Saul in your life and relate to David. As the Israelites, and Saul's son and daughter Michal, favored David more and more, Saul's anger turned to hate. Saul, pretending to be favorable to David, offered his daughter Merab to be David's wife. Saul was attempting to manipulate David, wanting him to believe he was on David's team. But remember, Saul is on a team of one. His thoughts behind the offer were devious. He was hoping that David would take the bait and become a more outspoken warrior and go out into the battlefield and do something stupid, allowing the Philistines to kill him so Saul wouldn't have to. Again, jealous leaders will not allow subordinates to be successful. They will do devious, dishonest things in order to retain their title, even to the point of manipulating those closest to them, which is what Saul did. After offering Merab to be David's wife, he changed his mind at the last minute. How this must have broken her heart! After all, David was honored, handsome, brave and faithful. Who wouldn't want to be married to him? But good old dad, the jealous king, was only using her to get David killed. David's response to all this was one of humility. Imagine the young, successful man who is anointed to be king saying he is a "nobody" and shouldn't be the one to marry the king's daughter. A nobody? How can he say that? He's not a nobody! He's the next king of

Israel! Take note of this behavior as it is something you and I, as leaders, must remember.

Saul's prideful heart was so full of hate for David that he offered another daughter's hand to him. This time it was Michal. David again wondered how he, a nobody, could be the king's son-in-law. This is hard to grasp. Humility is astounding. It goes against everything our flesh says to do. Again, Saul was hoping the Philistines would kill David. This did not happen. Quite the opposite, in fact. When a leader is so full of resentment, he not only wants his successor, or whoever is threatening him, to fail that he is willing to do anything to make that happen.

Now Saul was in a really hard spot. He messed up marriage number one, arranged and went through with marriage number two, and still David wasn't dead. So he turned to his son Jonathan, David's best friend. He outright asked him to kill David. No more plans forged in secret. Now it was out in the open. Saul wanted David dead. Jonathan is like so many who are put in this position. He had the not-so-glorious job of trying to convince Saul that David was not who he thought him to be. This is the same spot that the turtle in the bottom of the stack in Dr. Seuss's story found himself in. What a horrible place to be in. It is disheartening when leaders get to this place and won't listen to those closest to them, even family members. I wish it were not so. When leaders choose to be a team of one, they climb their leadership ladder and become so out of touch with reality that no one can convince them to come back down until it's too late and they come crashing down.

Saul's life ended tragically and painfully because he

allowed his pride to rule his actions and it ate him alive. David was an ExO leader and reigned as king and died with honor because his humility served him well. Every leader, whether he has a title or not, has a choice whether he will lead out of pride or humility. There is no in between. It is either one or the other. The same hand that anointed David removed Saul. Two kings. Two different outcomes. The proud king fell from his ladder with dishonor. The humble king was respected and honored. One was building his own kingdom, the other was building God's kingdom.

The fastest way to destroy a team is through pride. When a leader does what Matthew 23:4-8 says, which is always wanting the most visible position, the perks, the honorary degrees so you have extra letters attached to your signature, and the spot light on you, then you are allowing and encouraging people to put you on a pedestal. Watch out! The fall from that height is painful. Instead, work toward humility. Don't let people elevate you. As a Christian, Jesus is the One who should be elevated. But our inward desire for attention, which we wrongly equate as value, keeps us from the pursuit of humility. Matthew 23:11-12 continues the thought by telling those who have allowed themselves to be placed on a pedestal to get down and be a servant. Easier said than done. Oh how we love the publicity. It's so fun to see your name on the letterhead, on the CD cover, under the sermon title in the podcast or on the front of a book. But when those blessings come your way, what things are you doing to combat the lure of pride? One of the fastest ways I have found to combat pride is by volunteering. This is what I call "How to stay little."

How to stay little

This might seem like a peculiar thing to say, but to be an ExO leader, you have to stay little. Although your position may be large, your influence global, and your web of contacts endless, you will only inflate to proportions you will be unable to handle, sometimes causing failure, unless you plan to be little. There are many ways to become inflated, but there are equally as many ways to become little. One word: volunteer. That's it. Volunteer your time, without pay. Have you ever given your time at the homeless shelter? How about at your child's school, or the women's shelter or juvenile detention center? What organization, beside yours, needs you?

When you take time to volunteer, you are not only helping your community or church, you are helping yourself. There are three reasons why volunteering is healthy. First *you are opening yourself up to see someone else's needs*. It's so easy to get on our own speedway and expect everyone else to move out of our way so we can get the checkered flag. When you volunteer, things slow down and your vision is much different, which brings us to the second way you help yourself through volunteering.

Secondly, *offering your services to people or organizations through volunteering puts you into someone else's vision for a short period of time*. It puts you in the place of the unknown and the need to be dependent on someone else's expertise. You are no longer the top dog and become subordinate to someone else. This is healthy for many reasons.

When a leader gets accustomed to being the one

with all the knowledge, it's easy to move into a place of arrogance, expecting to be served, rather than serving others. Not many leaders begin this way. It happens over time if allowed. Human nature is selfish and concerned with only one thing: me! As long as leaders are busy with "me," there isn't room for anyone else, unless they volunteer their time. Volunteering opens ones eyes to the reality within another organization. Beyond the corporate scope, it keeps you leading from a grass roots level. Once you leave the grass roots, you will be out of touch and it is easy and probable that your vision will not only take on a new form, but that new form will be off base from where you started, which would be the second reason volunteering is vital to an ExO leader.

When a leader "humbles" himself to give of his time elsewhere, it changes his view of life. It doesn't reduce vision, but has a way of giving a new perspective. It can renew the vision you already have, or give you a fresh one. Serving others who don't know you, don't know your position or your power, will bring out various feelings in a leader. One emotion could be one of amazement. If you are a leader who likes to be served and find that as a volunteer you are the one serving others instead, you may be amazed at how good it feels to give back. You may also have a negative emotion of disgust in which you can't believe "these people" don't know who you are and the sacrifice it takes for you to be there. That would be even more cause for you to volunteer because it is healthy for you to be without a title for a short period of time. It has a way of weeding out arrogance and truly allowing a humble, servant-hearted leader to surface. In this place of service, you don't have to be called "sir," or "pastor" or "Mrs." What's your first name? That will do just fine.

There is a movie titled, "The Second Chance," written by Steve Taylor. It is a story of a mega church and an inner city church that they planted. The pastor of the inner city church, Jake, was formally the youth pastor for the pastor of the mega church. As the mega church grew, they became publicity hungry and used the inner city church to advertise their image. At the mega church, the pastor's son, Ethan, was the worship pastor. For publicity reasons, he invited Jake to come to his church on a Sunday morning take up an offering for the inner city work. It didn't go as well as planned. Out of disgust for their publicity hungry behavior, Jake threw an offering envelope at the first row of people. Ethan was now in trouble and was put on probation as the board led with a corporate mentality. They were attempting to clip his wings in order to prepare him to take his dad's place as pastor of this mega church.

With much objection, Ethan went to Jake's inner city church to volunteer. He hated every minute of it. His fancy car was his only comfort. In walking into a men's small group meeting at the inner city church, Ethan didn't receive immediate attention, as he would have at his dad's church. They didn't know his name, his title or his dad. He didn't know what to do. At one point, he had to volunteer at a homeless shelter and serve food. Of course cameras from his church were there to get further publicity.

In time, Ethan's heart began to melt for the people he was serving. It took time. At first, he didn't understand why the prostitute didn't just stop her behavior. He didn't understand why the Jr. high boy was allowing his older brother to use him to peddle drugs. There were a lot of things he didn't understand, until he volunteered.

By the end of his probation at Jake's church, Ethan's view of life was completely altered. He no longer desired to be a part of the publicity, the image and corporate mentality that his dad's church functioned in. He was forced to see life someone else's way, and in this situation, it changed more than anyone counted on. Ethan eventually allowed compassion to rule his behavior instead of a board of power hungry people. His probation made him into an ExO leader because when he volunteered, he could see the pain in people's lives and reach those who needed love. Sometimes it takes a major jolt for this to happen. Volunteering is one way for change to come to your heart, paving the way for you to lead the ExO way.

The last reason volunteering is healthy is because as a volunteer, *you are forced to get to know and understand someone else's vision and way of doing things.* You cannot walk into a room and demand of anyone. It's not your vision that is controlling the program. It's very helpful to a leader to experience this every now and then. It's freeing, actually. It gets your mind off your vision and is an avenue for you to give back to your community. At the same time you cannot promote yourself or your business while volunteering. A volunteer willingly serves. If while serving you would begin to promote yourself, it wouldn't take long and you'd either have to quit or be asked to leave. I have always loved hearing what other volunteers are busy doing outside of the time they are freely giving. It is amazing what they are giving up in order to serve. Some have other businesses they are running. Others are teachers that always have stacks of things to get through. Still others are busy keeping up with household duties or going to college. Volunteers are a unique group of people committed to a cause bigger than themselves: the cause of serving.

Having been a part of several volunteer groups, I have found a common thread in each one: they all work hard, as though they are being paid to be there. It is astounding to watch. When someone has willingly given of their time to serve, it does something that a title or a paycheck cannot do. I strongly urge you to seek out a place where you can volunteer your time, whether it's an after school program, a nursing home or a shelter.

The battle will be your time, but people make time for what's important, so the bigger battle will be your effort. If your company cannot do without you for two hours every other Thursday, that is possibly revealing something about your leadership which could be that you have given yourself too much control and it's time to train some of your team to take parts of the vision and make it happen. Chances are, they have been waiting in your shadow for this opportunity. It takes a humble leader to pass on responsibilities. Have you evaluated your level of humility lately?

Humility Evaluation

It is vital to leaders to do evaluations of several kinds. One key evaluation has to do with humility. There are a few ways to evaluate your level of humility.

1. Notice how considerate you are to others.
Does the language or attitude you carry in your tone of verbiage reflect a genuine care for others, or is it

flippant and casts a shadow on their value? To discover the answer it may take a painful step forward, such as an evaluation given to your team so they can help you reach a goal of health or just being healthier.

2. Are worried about your reputation?

This is when a leader is more concerned with what people think *of them* rather that what people see *in them*. Being worried about a reputation causes leaders to hide who they really are, limiting their success. If a leader is more concerned with their personal reputation than about having a humble heart, the team around him will build up the team of one. A healthy team doesn't have a desire to build up a leader. They have a desire to play a part in building a path to the team goal, allowing all team members to play their part.

3. Notice how well you handle criticism.

When was the last time you admitted a mistake, either publicly or privately? There can be admittance of wrongdoing, but for the wrong reasons, believe it or not. False humility can tell you to apologize, but then display self-pity, bringing the attention back on yourself, which is pride. Someone who does not admit any wrongdoing is full of pride and cannot be trusted. We all know that every human being has sinned. If we, as leaders, do not readily admit when we have messed up, then those on our teams cannot and should not trust us, as we are more concerned with our reputations than in being humble and truthful. The opposite of criticism is praise. Who wouldn't want to receive praise, or compliments and validation? You can check your humility by how you handle praise. Mark 10:17 gives us a quick, but revealing glance at Jesus' humility. A rich young ruler has come to Jesus and wants to know how to have eternal life. When he approached Jesus, he called Him a "good teacher." Jesus didn't take the compliment and allow pride to take root. Of course He was sinless and you and I are not. To follow His example, we ought to say what Jesus said, which was, "There is no one good but God." If anyone would have had a right to receive that compliment, it would have been Jesus. But the purpose for deflecting personal praise is to make sure we point people to God and to His goodness, not ours.

4. Notice who you surround yourself with.

Are they people who always agree with you? Insecure leaders, who are also prideful, like to hear only the good things. This does not allow for any healthy conflict or room to grow. Also, are the people around you well known and just by being next to them they make you look good? In my line of work, I am often around people who are well known in particular Christian circles. How easy it would be to drop names or shun those whose names aren't famous. But these wonderful speakers and music artists are human just like me. We all have the same Creator, were saved by the same Savior, and breathe the same air. There may be some who would want to be treated like they are in Hollywood. I love to give gifts, take care of my guests, and bless people. It's one of my favorite things to do. But one thing we should never do is put any person on a pedestal, giving him the glory that only Jesus deserves. Idol worship is not recommended. In fact, it's highly prohibited.

In the same right, you should never surround yourself only with people who depend on your guidance. This will give them the opportunity to put you on a pedestal. Not only that, it is also an avenue where pride can find it's way into your life by deceiving yourself into thinking your voice is more important to them than is the Holy Spirit's voice. This is a dangerous place for a leader to be. Ezekiel 14 talks directly to leaders who have idols in place of God. Without mercy and repentance, it doesn't end well. So the answer is this: surround yourself with a myriad of people. Some need you, some don't. Some will be your closest friends, others won't. Make sure there is someone who lifts your vision higher. Still others can hold you accountable. Balance is sure to come with a calico of people around you.

So how are you pursuing humility? There is no room in the kingdom of God for pride. What steps of action are you taking to not exalt yourself? This can be hard for a leader, especially a very successful leader. Finding humility in success takes purposeful steps away from pride and toward humility. James 4:6 says, "God resists the proud but gives grace to the humble." I don't know about you, but I need a lot of grace given to me. I need grace to persevere though this life. I need grace to live in God's spirit and not my flesh. I need His grace to keep Him as my focus. Without His grace, I can't be an ExO leader.

One example of humility is from the life of twelve year old Jesus, Emmanuel: God With Us. Even at twelve years old, Jesus knew He was God and He was among those He came to teach, save and heal. In Luke 2:39-52 we read the story of Jesus and his parents traveling to Jerusalem for Passover. While there, Jesus ended up in the temple, sharing deep truths with scholars and priests. They were amazed at what He revealed to them. The boy Jesus made sense of the puzzle pieces in the scriptures.

He talked and He asked questions. Somehow He lost track of time and somehow, His parents left town without him! Oops.

When they found him, three days later, they were understandably upset. They wondered why He was so irresponsible. His rebuttal was with a question. He wondered why they didn't know He would be about His father's business. This Jr. Higher was growing into a young man and was exercising his manhood as God made into flesh. He could have thumbed his holy nose at His parents and told them to go back home because He was busy doing God's work. If you read the entirety of the story, He did just the opposite. He obeyed, humbled Himself to his parental authority, and went home to be the carpenter's son.

He could have said many things, such as, "These are the people I came to save! I'm busy doing what I came to do, now go on home and let me be God." Can you imagine? Humility in Jesus told Him to submit and go home. God exalts the humble in the proper time (1 Peter 5:4).

Jesus also exemplified humility when He washed His disciples feet (John 13:1-20). Imagine Emmanuel washing dirt and sweat off feet that He created. How much more we need to follow His example of not climbing a ladder. Instead, we need to stay close to the dirt because you never know when He's going to ask you to wash some feet, hold an orphan, cry with a drug addict, or serve food to the homeless. This is what we call "servant leadership."

Servant Leadership

In Matthew 20:25b-28 Jesus said this: "...You know that the rulers of the Gentiles lord it over them, and their high officials exercise authority over them. Not so with you. Instead, whoever wants to become great among you must be your servant, and whoever wants to be first must be your slave - just as the Son of Man did not come to be served, but to serve, and to give his life as a ransom for many."

You can take your leadership to another level just by serving. This is not a program change. It's a heart change. If you want to be a great leader, start by serving those around you. An awesome thing will happen – your desire to be served will fade away! On the same note, serving to be seen by others is also prideful. This kind of behavior quickly turns into performance. Matt. 6:1-2(MSG) puts it this way: "Be especially careful when you are trying to be good so that you don't make a performance out of it. It might be good theater, but the God who made you won't be applauding. When you do something for someone else, don't call attention to yourself." It is spiritually irritating when leaders flaunt their good works, whether it's in a corporate or private setting. Just because he gave money to a homeless man, because God told him to and he obeyed, does not mean it needs to end up in a sermon. Sometimes, it's more important to allow the lesson learned, or the opportunity given by God, to remain between those involved. You have an audience of one. One, with a capital "O."

Just as wanting to be served instead of serving is prideful, self-sufficiency, also a form of pride. It says that you can't be served. This includes being "served" a new way of doing things. The prideful leader becomes unteachable. How can a leader effectively reach his team if he cannot be served and he doesn't want to learn from anyone? He can't. He will be ineffective. What looks like humility is really self-sufficiency and a reliance on oneself instead of on God. This spells disaster for a team. In Mark 10:35-44 we read the story of two of Jesus' disciples, James and John asked Jesus an astounding question. They had arrived at a comfortable place in their relationship with Jesus and boldly asked if He could reserve the "highest seats of honor" in heaven, those on Jesus' left and right, for them. We could judge their question, but not without examining our own hearts first. So before you or I judge them, let's finish the story. Jesus knew they couldn't die for the sins of the world like He was about to do, so he offered another way to get to those high seats of honor. He said it wasn't going to happen the way the religious leaders of the day were doing it, which was throwing their religious weight around and letting their power go to their heads. Instead, He said that whoever wants the best seats needs to become a servant, which is what He came to do. So basically He was saying, "Follow my example and you will be honored." But in order to follow His example, it will take humility and servant hood, which more times than not, is a difficult road. It requires that we go against our need for approval from man and seek God's approval. Remember, we have an audience of One.

Finally, a leader who deals with pride will feel and behave as though he is entitled to more. Depending on your situation, this will look different for everyone. But the result is the same: a demanding leader. Many leaders have gone through very difficult trials because of pride. You may have been that leader, or you may have worked for that leader. We will close the book with that topic, but for now allow me to encourage you to take a moment and check the motivation of your life. It's worth it!

Out of the Box Vision

You see, I am passionate about your becoming all you can be, and to see your workplace become all it was dreamed to become. Someone, somewhere had a vision. Can you fulfill their vision? Maybe it's your vision. You carry the heart for it, but you must pass it on with health. If you put the vision in a box, it will die.

Picture a box. Now picture yourself in it. Climb in that box and close the lid. What do you see? That's right – nothing. There are no holes for light to get in. Does anything grow in the dark? Yes: mold. Do you want your vision in a box to just get moldy and die? On the same note, when someone dies we lay them in a box, close the lid and bury them. When you put your vision in a box, you aren't giving life to it. It's not available for anyone to touch. It's protected, guarded, and without any new ideas being added to it, it will die in that darkness. Vision needs to be out in the open with your team speaking life into it. Take that lid off! Let others share in the creation of it. That's healthy! The leader is the lid, like a ceiling, that keeps your team from going any higher, or you can remove yourself from being the lid, allowing your team to have unlimited success.

Vision is doing the thing that needs to be done,

even if you are pioneering your way through it. Be flexible and let the journey take you to new heights. As you sojourn with your team, you will be planting markers that many others behind you will follow. Do your best to lead the right and healthy way.

Potluck Leading

Think of vision casting like a potluck. It's a planned opportunity for many creative things to happen. There are a few pointers we can take from them.

1. Everyone brings something to the table, such as their creativity and abilities.
When a planned opportunity is made available, it allows for the people on your team to bring their ideas to the table. Healthy leaders allow for this type of meeting to take place. Unhealthy leaders feel intimidated, or even threatened by this type of meeting. A leader who is non-aggressive will feel intimidated because of all the ideas, opinions and dreams of others. He doesn't know what to do with them and shrinks back in fear, being paralyzed and unable to take action. An authoritative leader feels threatened by these ides, opinions and dreams. This is simply because he is not able to control them. If he gives his team any room to express their thoughts, he fears they may take over the entire team, which would take authority away from him. A healthy leader welcomes the diverse opinions of his team. He recognizes their need to vocalize those opinions, goals and dreams. He also understands that in order for his team to be healthy and strong, this must take place.

2. Don't focus on what's not there.

Take the opportunity to create with your team. Dream up what you don't see and watch your team take the initiative to "build" it. Not everything is going to be tasty. You may find out that some things weren't as good as originally thought. That happens, so move on. Don't park on the mistakes, but learn from them. Give your team some room to grow, which also means room to make mistakes. One mark of a healthy leader is allowing his team to make mistakes comfortably.

3. Just because it looks good doesn't mean you should eat it.

Not every idea is a good idea. I love to cook and bake in my kitchen. Because I am comfortable there, many ideas easily flow. There have been times, in my comfort zone, when some of those ideas didn't turn out so good. I fed the garbage disposal rather than my family. They didn't fire me. I was given the room to make those things I thought looked good. But once those dreams became reality, it was obvious we wouldn't be eating my amazing creation. The point is this: allow your team to dream, but remember that some things they come up with won't be all it was imagined to be. A healthy leader is okay with that.

4. A potluck isn't just about the food, but about getting together to build relationship.

You can't have healthy vision casting without relationship building, just like you can't have a potluck without having conversations with people. You can't force someone to eat the spaghetti with meatballs. But if you dialogue about it, chances are they may willingly try a little bit. Because you didn't force it on them, they may be willing to at least hear you. When a leader isn't forceful, but is understanding, the team will be more workable and willing to try new things. If team building is based on relationship building, the sky is the limit.

Leadership can be a lot of fun. Having a team of people to lead doesn't have to be overwhelming. Doing a few simple things can change your entire outlook. According to Solomon, who had everything a human could want, the work wasn't all that fun when he stepped back and saw that there wasn't anyone to pass it on to. He realized there is a time for everything and working yourself and others to death doesn't prove anything. Being busy doesn't mean we're "better" than the person who takes time off. Taking a "subordinate" to coffee is a better option. Solomon comments on this in Ecclesiastes 3:12-13 by saying, "I know that there is nothing better for men than to be happy and do good while they live. That everyone may eat and drink, and find satisfaction in all his toil – this is a gift of God."

Did he just say a "gift of God?" Most people like gifts. Gifts are personal. There are times you and I have been given a gift that was more about the giver than the receiver. The gift was something the giver would wear, or would put in their house, but it was far from your decorating style or your favorite color. No one likes those gifts. It's a reflection on the giver. It shows a bit of selfishness on their part. So what kind of gift is Solomon talking about? It's the ability to enjoy your work, as well as those who work for you, and to be satisfied in all you do. You have been given special talents. As you allow your leadership to be refined, you will enjoy the work of your hands.

Sometimes the work of a leader's hands isn't above the table, so to speak. An unhealthy leader tends to make the work of their hands into a tool to build up their own kingdom. There are some leaders who appear to enjoy the high seat of authority they've either been given, or they have awarded to themselves. But that is until they get knocked off their tower of glory. It is at that time when they have a choice to make whether or not they will lead differently. It takes an inward change to see and receive the gift of enjoying your work and finding satisfaction in it.

My deepest heart's desire as a leader is to see lives changed because of the influence Jesus has in my life and how I can pass that influence onto others. I remember the day when a mom of one of the teens in our youth group called and desperately asked me to meet regularly with her high school aged daughter who was deep into an eating disorder. I was honored to step in and help. For a few years I met from time to time with this young woman, watching her go up and down, finally making a turn towards health and wholeness. She met a young man and fell in love. My husband and I had the pleasure of doing their pre-marriage counseling and participating in their wedding! As wonderful as all of that was, the moment that a brought tear to my eye was the day this newly married friend and I had coffee together. She told me how she and her husband had been meeting with another couple who were dating. My friend told me some of the things she was sharing with this couple. I couldn't contain my emotion. Hearing this young woman pass on the things I'd spoken into her life was such a reward! I was overwhelmed to see those nuggets passed on. *That* is the reward all leaders should strive for. That can't happen if you are on a ladder. Get down where the people are. They need you and they need what you humbly have to offer them. This didn't happen in front of a crowd. It was just she and I in the corner of a small coffee shop. No applause, no podcast, no power point presentation with heart-warming music - just a moment of gratitude for someone who took what I'd given and passed it on.

Kingdom mentality

It's never too late to start a new way of living. If it's not part of your DNA, it will be nothing but deceit, and there's nothing a person dislikes more than a fraud. If you're going to change as a person and then as a leader, make sure it's for the right reasons. Make sure it's to build the "Big K," that is, God's kingdom, not yours. It's so rewarding! At one critical point in my life, God asked me whose kingdom I was building up, His, mine or the devil's. I had to stop and think about it. I had graduated from cosmetology college and was at a point of decision. I was either going to try and move to Minneapolis and join the Rocco Altobelli salon, or try and get into music. I though making it big in the hair business, and possibly becoming an instructor would be a lot of fun. I also wanted to become either a backup singer and travel with recording artists, or be a singer/songwriter. God knew just what to say and when. After examining my life, I knew what I was supposed to do. I went to Bible college. I was supposed to allow my own dreams to die and take up God's dream He had for my life. His dream is to build His kingdom through me. As long as I was building my own kingdom, I wasn't building His. I could have let the words of affirmation from my instructors at cosmetology school point me in the wrong direction. They said I would go far with my talent. I was the top of my class and continued to excel. On my first haircut at school, my instructor didn't have to correct any of it. She just kept combing, trying to find something to cut. She finished and told my first client that she'd received a perfect haircut. I was very excited and began to have hopes of going far in that profession. But God had other plans of which I submitted to.

God allowed me to do something I'd wanted to do since I was three years old and putting barrettes in my dad's hair. God gifted me to accomplish my goal and to succeed at it. To be honest with you, I knew deep down inside that I was to be in ministry to teenagers. God called me to that at fifteen years of age. But my idea of what it looked like and how God viewed it were two different things. I could have let the positive reinforcement about my cosmetology skill change me and redirect my paths. Equally as troubling, I could have let it change me. I could have become proud and arrogant. Some students in cosmetology school even commented to me that the instructors favored me. In other words, I was the teacher's pet. I didn't see that side of it. I didn't want to be noticed that way. I just wanted to stay in my little corner and do what I loved doing.

Too often people change so they are more accepted, or so they are more significant. Those changes aren't real. It has to be who you are in the long line at the driver's license office. It has to be who you are at your child's school or their sports activities. Being a leader isn't easy. It's a gift that spills out on people and we need to learn how to contain the spillage and use what we know wisely. I was able to minister to one student next to my station. While we worked on our mannequins, she would ask me spiritual questions. This was more important to me than my mannequin. It was a choice to stay God-focused. We all face this choice throughout our lifetimes. And as leaders, this choice comes up often.

The big question is what will you do with the gifts God has given you? It takes insight from God to walk into your future. If you do it alone, you will end up building either your own kingdom or the devil's. Proverbs 28:26 (MSG) says, "Among leaders who might lack insight, abuse abounds, but for the one who hates corruption, the future is bright." If you are building your kingdom, you will use and abuse people with your leadership. This builds the devil's kingdom because your actions come from a prideful heart.

Your future is bright, as long as you allow your leadership style to be examined, even allowing criticism to shape you into being the healthiest leader you can be. You have a bright future filled with fulfillment, as you allow yourself the opportunity to change where it's needed. So begin with some reflection on what you've read.

Those in leadership are gifted people. They bring unity to a team, and keep the door of success open and limitless. We, as leaders, have the platform to either lead people to success, or we can lead them into dead end paths. Jesus, in Matthew 25, tells us how to not only live, but how to lead. He says that when we feed the hungry, give drink to the thirsty, give shelter to the homeless, give clothes to the naked, and visit those who are sick and those who are imprisoned, we are actually doing them to Jesus because those are His people too.

If you notice, every one of those actions is an outward action. None of them are beneficial to the one doing the action. They are all "others oriented." When the dark side of a leader comes out, those actions are brought into the open in order for that leader to be praised for those "self-less" actions, thus turning a good deed into a selfish deed. What wonderful opportunities we have all around us to touch people through all those avenues, and knowing we are doing them unto Jesus is even better yet! God's kingdom doesn't look like we make it look sometimes. We get more wrapped up in what color the carpet of the new auditorium should be, or the color of the paint in the pastor's office. Get the paint and carpet picked out and get back to work in doing the things that really matter, as described in Matthew 25.

How are you leading your team to be others oriented? Are you doing any of those things listed in Matthew 25? If so, are you doing them for show or are you quietly, without praise, doing them for Jesus?

This would be a good time for you to do a couple of things: You could write out your thoughts and leave it there. Or, you could write out your thoughts and make a game plan. If you realize what you've been doing hasn't been working, and you see a little bit of the unhealthy leader in yourself, then you need to make some goals on how you're going to change. But wait! There's more! It can't end there. You will need someone in your life that will help you meet these goals. As I mentioned earlier, if there is no accountability, change will not come. You will soon forget what you've learned and go back to the way you've always led.

The leaders around you need *you* to change. They need you to be accountable to someone, as this will bring new life to them. Not only will you change as a leader at your job, but as a husband and father, as a mother and wife. These changes are not just work related – they are internal, like your DNA.

This is not a quick fix, but a journey towards change. As you change, you will see how others respond to you. They will have grace for this change, and they will be your biggest fans! So don't give up. Keep walking, running and sometimes sprinting to the goals you've set. Your success is not in how fast you run, but in how faithful you are in the race.

You may be wondering where you can begin your change. I suggest you begin with your overall view of what "team" means to you? Do you view the team as a group of people who work *for* you or who work *with* you? Everyone wants to be a part of something that is successful. They want to feel like they have been given a voice on the team and share in the success of the team. They are also there to help find a solution for what didn't work. Leading a team means you are willing to hear their concerns, dreams, hopes, and even their criticism. It means you are willing to open up your life and be vulnerable to break down the wall that you may have built up to retain your authority. Remember that *one cannot be an ExO leader without being relational.* To explore how relational you are, how do you carry yourself in the office? It's not about the suit you wear or the professional code of conduct you follow. Rather, it's about how you conduct yourself within those parameters. It can be easy for a professional to hide behind the tie or the heels, all while attempting to maintain undary between them and the other leaders under n. Boundaries have a place, but they should not be d to maintain your power as a leader. This only creates tance, misunderstanding and stress in the workplace.

One way to be relational is to notice a few simple things around the office. Take for instance how things are arranged. Are the chairs arranged in a meeting type of arrangement or are they conducive to a sit-down conversation? Does your office look approachable or does it look breakable? This is where the relational experience begins. It will pay off for your team and for you personally. Everyone wins with this type of leading.

Begin to come out of your office and socialize from time to time. Let those around you get to know you. This is the only way you will be an influence on them. They know who the leader is; they just need to get to know the leader. This will take some time. You need time to figure it out and so do those around you. This could be very uncomfortable for a leader who has led with control. It may seem like you are giving your control or authority away, but for those around you, it is welcomed.

For about a month, I was working with a team of people who traveled an hour to a private residential resort on the side of a mountain to clean the homes of multi-millionaires. Our boss was a strong Christian man. He was a quiet and kind man. But being a Christian does not make one a good leader. I did not choose to work with this team because of the boss. But after working with this team and my boss, I learned a lot about leadership and letting go of control.

Imagine you have signed contracts to take teams of

people into homes that are worth millions of dollars. The owners and the agencies you contracted with trust you and your team to not ruin anything, jeopardize the owner's privacy or steal anything. If you were the boss with this kind of pressure, how would you manage your team? Most of us would pull out the control card and play it to the point of running off every worker we had.

My boss, Matt, didn't do that. He was a gracious leader who allowed us to be who we were, to function as individuals but work as a team. That may not seem to make sense, so let me explain.

When I first joined the team, the very first home we went to was owned by someone who made you sign a contract promising that you could not tell anyone whose home you were working at in order not to jeopardize their home, their family or their riches. Matt did not tell me where we were at until we were standing on the property. He didn't make a big deal out of it, but gave me a pen to sign the contract. He didn't take me aside and go through the dos and don'ts of cleaning this mansion. He gave me the boundaries and let me get to work. He did not follow me around, looking over my shoulder to see if I was obeying the contract I signed. He didn't spy on me to make sure I wasn't taking pictures with my cell phone or rummaging through drawers to find cash (the hidden security cameras took care of that). Matt allowed me to find my way, ask questions when necessary and get the job done. I was functioning as an individual, but was quickly learning how to gel with the team under his leadership. There was no stress. There were no outrageous expectations, just simple guidelines with room to grow.

You see, a leader who leads with control leaves no room for growth in his team. If the leader already has all the strings in his hand, then the workers, or staff is unable to make a move without their leader moving them. That puts a lot of stress and responsibility on the leader that doesn't seem necessary, or productive for this controlling leader. The worker becomes unproductive and learns to work only when told how to, limiting his productivity and creativity.

Matt also contracted his team to do construction clean up at brand new multi-million dollar homes. We were responsible to clean up all the dust particles left behind. That means even the timbers 20 feet up, the huge rock fireplaces, and the rock walls. Every rock, timber, nook and cranny was to be dusted, wiped down and made ready for the owners to inspect upon arrival, or prepared for the interior decorators. In order for this to be accomplished, it took a healthy leader. At times, Matt wasn't even at the work site, as he needed to be at other sites directing the other teams of people, and also working just as hard as anyone else.

It seems endless what we, as leaders, can achieve. But somehow, we've got to realize that it's not about power, authority or position that get us to those heights. We've got to realize that it's not the job of our staff or employees, to hold us up, enabling us to succeed.

"Nearly all men can stand adversity, but if you want to test a man's character, give him power."

Abraham Lincoln

ExO 3
ExO Style

It does not require one to read hours and hours of books, take college courses or be at the top of his class with straight A's to be an ExO leader. All it takes is willingness to not only change, but also a willingness to invest in the lives of others. A healthy leader knows how to think of others needs, visions and values. It's not just about the leaders vision, but the team vision as a whole. A healthy leader knows how to implement everyone's desires and goals into the vision. It's not the leaders job to make everyone happy. Rather, it is the leaders job to make sure everyone's voice has been heard and they have been validated. If a leader is not a team driven leader, he runs the risk of disbanding whatever team may have been in place and will be left having all decisions rise *and fall* on him alone.

The Team Driven Leader

This leader is not threatened with the opinions of others. In fact, he welcomes them. He seeks the thoughts of those on his team. He sees the value of his team and leans on their ideas and suggestions. This leader is the final authority, but does not make decisions alone; He uses the strength of the entire team to build the company, or the organization, based on the vision he has laid out for them. The entire team holds to that vision, with the values and principles of that company or organization as their guide. He is respected for his role, as he has given respect to those under him. He has validated their thoughts and concerns.

There is an open door to him and the leaders in his care are safe with him. They know they can approach him with anything and he will give them the dignity and respect their relationship requires. In this type of leader, there is confidence, not fear. *This confidence breeds bigger dreams*, as those dreaming are not afraid to speak up.

Here is an amazing concept: ask people to follow your leadership and they just come, without looking back. How does that happen? It starts with mutual respect. Granted, there are some people who will connect with you and others who won't. This disconnect is generally based on how you view other leaders. Do you view them as threats or do you see the leaders under you as an opportunity to change a life? When a young leader can be mentored into becoming a healthy leader, they will follow your leading. In fact, they will be your biggest advocates. When they feel a mutual respect, they will be the largest assets a leader could ever have. They will follow a good leader.

Leaders validate people and expand their talents

When you validate someone you value him. It's an acceptance of their individuality, not an agreement with their opinions. Validation gives people a safe place to share their opinions. When a person feels safe, they can, in essence, spread their wings and fly. Their talents will be expanded because validation will give them the room and the freedom to grow. As long as validation is not being used to manipulate, people thrive in this kind of environment. Your favorite teacher from your school years is most likely the one who validated you. He or she gave you verbal pats on the back, which gave you confidence to learn the things you didn't think you could, and gave you the persistence to reach goals that seemed out of reach. As an adult, you are no different now than you were then. You are still human and that requires the need for validation.

There are times when we get restless with life. It's hard to expand our talents when we feel like a tiger in a cage. It is at that juncture a healthy leader can step in and say, "Hey, I love the way you do your job. Have you thought about doing it this way? Let me help you. I think we can make a big difference in this community if we do this together." Saying it that way verses, "I've been thinking," (as the pencil taps on the yellow legal paper notebook in their hands), "you have been here for quite a while. I think it's time you do your job this way instead. Here's a plan I've laid out for you. I need you to do this and we'll talk in three months from now. I believe in you."

I apologize if this offends you, but that is a lame way to lead. Lame means unable to walk due to an illness. It is impossible to lead people to greatness if we, as leaders, are ill ourselves. To become a healthy, ExO leader requires a willingness to notice the talents in those around you, and showering them with validation.

Vision

An ExO leader is a visionary. He can see where the team needs to go. But that isn't all he needs. An ExO leader needs to know how to implement the visions of those on his team and how to involve their talents to make it happen. A vision is not just a dream that happened one day. When someone has a vision, it feels like it's the purpose for which they were born. Most people are quite passionate about their visions. The trouble comes when a leader forges forward without the unity of his team, or their talents to make that vision a reality. There are a few things you need to realize before casting your vision.

1. Vision casting creates dialogue.
When you cast vision, meaning you present your vision in full detail, it will create a moment when those on your team will want to dialogue about it, adding their vision to yours. When you release your vision to your team, you release your ownership of it. That does not mean it's up for grabs. What it does mean is you trust your team with it. As you allow them to speak into it, adding their perspective, you are showing them respect and value their thoughts, whether they fully agree or disagree with your vision. This is a very crucial time for a team. If you are a threatened leader, this will be very uncomfortable for you. In fact, if it doesn't go well, your team may unravel and dismantle. When you are ready to cast vision, allow for dialogue, opinions and dreams to come from your team. Just as when a transcript goes to an editor, there are many things

that need adjusting and changing. Don't expect your original vision to be the final outcome. Expect changes to happen. In fact, a secure and healthy leader will encourage changes and refinement of his vision. Guide your team to a place of unity, making sure everyone has been heard and validated.

2. Vision casting creates tension.

Not everyone is going to agree with what you see. Some on your team may stand directly opposed to it. How are you going to handle that? The key to working through tension is listening with a purpose. Don't let a team member drone on and on. Listen to them with your ears tuned into key things they are saying. They may have had a bad experience in the past and are reliving it through your newly casted vision. This would also mean they are working through fear from that negative event. Be patient with them and listen intently to them. There may be others who could be jealous of your new vision, wishing they'd thought of it first and so they will oppose it no matter what. This will require a private meeting with this team member. Don't air their laundry at a vision-casting meeting. Take notes and meet with them over coffee later. Don't allow their negative words cast a shadow on your team. Curb it and move the team past it as quickly as you can. There will be others who will ask some tough and legitimate questions about your vision. Welcome that type of dialogue. If you have a good team, they will be passionate and ready to express it. Allow for positive tension to happen. It is proper for you, the leader, to ask your team to help you build this vision. If you bring it to them already set in stone, you are just a team of one. But if you open it up and allow their voice to be heard, even if they disagree with you, your team will support and stand behind you.

3. Vision casting brings opportunity.

Your first thought may be that this opportunity is for the team to be a part of your exciting vision. But *my* first thought is how beneficial vision casting is for you, the leader of this team. In creating an opportunity for your well thought out vision to be heard, you have also created a place of feedback. That is an opportunity for you to hear the thoughts and concerns of your team. It is an open door into their thoughts. What you do with that matters greatly. This opportunity will help shape you as a leader, as well as your team members. Take the opportunity you've given yourself to grow and capitalize on it. Take notes about what you see in your leadership. You may see some things you can change and do better next time. And yes, you have also brought opportunity to your team, allowing them to expand. Vision casting is an opportunity for all team members to discuss one common goal, but with many angles. An ExO leader loves angles. Imagine your vision like a sphere. When you present your vision, you are allowing your team to bring their thoughts like a bunch of arrows pointing directly at your vision (sphere). If that is scary to you, you may not want to release your vision yet. Their thoughts will pierce your sphere to test it and reshape it. The exciting thing is their fingerprints will be on your vision. God created the sphere we live on, but allows us to reshape it with our ideas, like landscaping in my yard. The basic structure will always be there, but how it looks will change. What a marvelous opportunity you are giving yourself and your team by vision casting!

4. Vision casting inspires.

John Quincy Adams said, "If your actions inspire others to dream more, learn more, do more and become more, you are a leader." If a team doesn't have goals higher than themselves they will only scatter. It doesn't take much to inspire a good team. Give them a goal and they will create the road to get there. The world changes when people are inspired. Without it, visions and dreams die. Inspiration causes ingenuity. When team members are given freedom to be creative, your vision will be formed into something unimaginable This is why having the right staff around you is vital. When you allow your vision to inspire them, the sky is the limit for your organization.

During his three and a half years of ministry on this earth, Jesus cast vision everywhere He went. His vision was that the world would know Him and His Father. Everything He did pointed back to that. Jesus inspired people with faith to do things greater than they'd done before, for the sake of the kingdom of God. Take for instance a situation accounted for in Mark 9:38-41. One of the twelve disciples, John, complained to Jesus about a man using Jesus' name to drive a demon out of someone. John said he and the other disciples stopped the man because he wasn't one of them. My frustration with their behavior stems from being on several teams who were very inspirational. That inspiration spread, as it should, to more than one team. When others get it, let them! Jesus was not about to stop this nameless man from doing good things, by faith in His name. Jesus knew how to release others to do even greater things than even He would do. He didn't control people like the religious leaders were known to do.

Release is described as a leader holding his team or staff in his cupped hands out in front of him. This would symbolize release, allowing the team to function free and independent of his control. But I find two flaws in this. First, at any moment, this leader's hands can fold in on the team and they are capped and crushed. Second, if the team is in cupped hands, they are not free to move around or dream. They are held within the control of this leader. Wherever the leader moves them, that is where they find themselves. If the team is not following the vision correctly, this leader can start to squeeze, putting pressure on his team to follow his lead. This is not productive or healthy. In the end, the team will burn out and leave and this leader will be left with empty hands. If you begin leading your team with empty hands, you won't ever be disappointed because your hands will always be full. They will be full of inspiration, dreams and goals given to you by your team. Holding tightly to a team is not what an ExO leader does.

    Might I suggest a slightly different way to release? Since a team does not belong to the leader, they are an entrustment given for a specific purpose and time, they ought to be in a released position. Instead of the team being in cupped hands, the leader's hands ought to be turned facing outward. This symbolizes no control, but an assurance that the right team has been chosen and they are free to function under his direction. When there is no shadows over them and no fear of collapse, they will move about with confidence and trust the leader and his vision.

    When you have an outward vision, you can train, or mentor your team into who they have been designed to be. *When people are validated you can take them to unknown heights in their talents.* Notice it's taking them to their talents and not yours. A leader is not called to make clones of themselves, but to help others become the best they can be in who they are and who they are becoming. This takes work on the leaders part. You have to pay attention and purposefully watch their lives. It can't be guess work. Matthew 23:15 gives great instruction on this matter. Here Jesus warned the religious teachers not to go around the world looking for people to make just like themselves. He told them matter-of-fact that clones would be worse than they were, and that was a bunch of hypocrites. What strong language! You and I need to take those words to heart. Are we doing what Jesus said not to do? The people on your team should act like Jesus more than they act like you as you lead them in that direction. When it's all said and done, what have you left your team with? If all you've left them is your name, then you haven't done your job. But if you've left an impression on them, rooted in the identity of Christ, then you've done an excellent job. If you have an eternal vision, you will be able to relinquish control and let people be who God intended them to be. Once vision is established in your team, the next milestone is trust.

Do people trust in your leadership?

Have you given them a reason to trust you? There are people who will come into your leadership circle. They are entrusted to you. Are you going to help them become the great leaders they are called to be, or is your concern about their support for you and your vision?

*An **apprentice** is someone who is being taught a trade; they are just beginning to learn something new.*

If you are currently an unhealthy leader, the word

apprentice might scare you. Unhealthy leaders tend to see it only their way. Why is this? I believe it is because of fear. If they allow others to get close to them, they would have to be relational. Being relational means being open and humble – it means being close to another. Remember, unhealthy leaders are on a vertical climb, which means they are by themselves. They have no intention to let you climb with them.

As a leader, do you intend to teach the young up and coming leaders entrusted to you? The point in being a leader is not to flex muscles of authority, but to pass on a dream. What dream are you cultivating in your team that will be passed on?

Solomon

In the Bible, you can read of the world's best "earthly" king, and that was King David. David raised a son names Solomon, who also became a King. Solomon was given the gift of wisdom. Now before you ask for that gift, you might want to know what a struggle it would be. Solomon's wisdom drove him to seek out knowledge and understanding, but as he repeatedly says, it all meant nothing. You might be wondering how that could be. After all, he gave his eyes all they desired, such as vast vineyards, outlandish gardens, massive reservoirs, illustrious parks, and had more wives than any one man can handle. But even then, he still wasn't satisfied.

To bring an answer to this dilemma, let's look at what Solomon said in Ecclesiastes 2:17-21 NIV.

"So I hated life, because the work that is done under the sun was grievous to me. All of it is meaningless, a chasing after the wind. I hated all the things I had toiled for under the sun, because I must leave them to the one who comes after me. And who knows whether he will be a wise man or a fool? Yet he will have control over all the work into which I have poured my effort and skill under the sun. This too is meaningless. So my heart began to despair over all my toilsome labor under the sun. For a man may do his work with wisdom, knowledge and skill, and then he must leave all he owns to someone who has not worked for it. This too is meaningless and a great misfortune."

When you, a gifted leader, guide and direct people to build what you see, it gives you pleasure to see it finished before your very eyes. Isn't that the goal? To Solomon, apparently not.

So what are your goals? The key is found in these words of Solomon: "But I must leave them to the one who comes after me. And who knows whether he will be a wise man or a fool? Yet he will have control over all the work into which I have poured my effort and skill under the sun." And again in these words: "For a man may do his work with wisdom, knowledge and skill, and then he must leave all he owns to someone who has not worked for it."

The heartache he pens is that he has toiled at making sure the things he sees in his head become a reality, but at the expense of not passing it on. He didn't mentor anyone to take it over when he was gone.

This is a very strategic moment in this book. It is at

this point that you and I need to stop and evaluate who we are as a leader. Do I really mentor others, or just make sure that all my plans succeed and they are just my servants? That is a very real issue in leaders. Far too often, leaders go to the level of being unhealthy because of this fact alone. All they see is what's in their head and they won't be satisfied until it's a reality. But as Solomon repeats time and time again, "This too is meaningless."

What purpose does it serve for you to build up your kingdom? Those plans and dreams you have in your head will need to come out, but when they do, there will be skilled and talented people around you to help make that happen. But your leadership skills are not just for that purpose. They are also there to help shape and mold those who are working for you because when you move on, they are the ones left behind to take over. They are the ones you poured into, not bossed around. They are the ones who will carry your vision, as well as intermingle it with the person you've helped them to become.

Jesus

Let's contrast Solomon's leadership with that of Jesus. It may not seem fair, since Jesus is God's sinless Son. But I want to point out the notable difference.

First of all, both Solomon and Jesus had a team of people around them who were gifted to get the job done. But the difference is this: Solomon told them to build what he saw without mentoring them in that vision. Instead he was task-oriented. That means that building the task took priority over building the people. He wanted them to build *his* kingdom. Because Jesus was people-oriented, He hand picked twelve men whom He knew he could mentor to follow His vision. Jesus knew His dream was safe with them and could confidently pass it on to them. His goal was to teach them to be kingdom minded. He needed to instill that kind of a vision in them. This built a foundation on which the church could grow. An organization can grow with those parameters. You can even take those same parameters and apply them to your home life. Don't attempt to make clones of yourself, but reproduce the vision you have for your family. When you are gone, they will continue to live by those principles, and within those parameters.

This type of leadership, requires relationship. Jesus spent time with His disciples. If you, either as a leader in your home or an organization, do not build relationship with those you are leading, your ability to be heard will be limited. Take for instance the way Jesus allowed His disciples to ask Him questions. He went out of His way to explain the meaning behind the parables He told others. He wanted them to get it. If they didn't get it, the foundation He was attempting to build would have been lost. In order to teach servanthood He had to practice it. He did this several times. The most memorable is when He washed the feet of His disciples (John 13).

Jesus also trained His disciples which involves participation. He wanted the disciples to participate in the activities He was implementing. It takes freedom in order for that to happen, whether centuries ago or present day. Allowing people to have the room they need to grow, learn and get involved is vital. Restricting people is not healthy leadership. Yes, there are times when the reigns get pulled back, giving those on your team the grace to grow through training. Train them toward the goal. What is it you need them to know? What kind of beliefs and behaviors are required for you to confidently hand the vision over to them? In order for that to happen, it will take your participation in their lives. Solomon didn't participate in the lives of others in order to pass on a vision or a dream. Jesus understood something that you and I as leaders need to understand. It's not about the dream. It's about the person.

It's not about the dream. It's about the person

It's about the journey to see the dream become a reality. This is what Solomon was so disappointed about in this portion of Scripture. He did all he could to satisfy his dream, but when he had it all in front of him, it meant nothing. There wasn't another person to see the vision continue.

Many people have unfulfilled dreams. There are outstanding dreams that most every leader could admit to. But just because you want to fulfill an unmet dream, doesn't mean you should. If being a leader is not about the dream but about the people, then you should pour into the leaders around you. Through them your dream can unfold. You would be busy working on lives, and not on the dream. It will happen through people. You may have the talents, the preparedness, the team and resources, but should you continue to accomplish your unfulfilled dream when your team isn't unified? If they aren't ready for your dream, or they just don't catch it, then what? Will you accomplish it through force, or a healthy development process? Prepare them to carry your vision through training and teaching.

In order to be the kind of person who is willing to pass on a dream, you *cannot* be a dictator. It's just not possible. Solomon says over and over throughout Ecclesiastes that everyone has the same ending: death. What does it gain you to be unhealthy? On the same token, just flip it over – what does it gain you to be healthy? Again, it's about relationship, teaching, and training. There will be times when those in your team make a wrong decision. Are you going to extend grace so they are able to continue growing and learning? At other times they will question your vision. How are you going to handle that? Out of relationship, they will be able to ask you tough questions. If you are not threatened by that, you will welcome those questions, seeing they are attempting to join your vision. If a team member has questions and is not allowed to ask them, he will become disgruntled and disunity will soon evolve. It would be tragic if a valuable team member resigned because the leader was threatened and would not allow healthy conflict to arise. It takes relationship and freedom to maintain unity on a team.

There is strength in unity

Unity provides everyone with a voice. It does not mean all the voices say the same thing. It does mean they all agree on forward motion. It means they agree to disagree. Unity is a roundtable: this is where everyone lays down their swords and agrees to be civil and has previously decided to walk away and be friends, no matter what. This is healthy conflict. When someone on the team says, "No," this is not a rejection of you, the leader. It's an opportunity to go in a different direction. Do you see the difference: Rejection vs. opportunity? If you feel rejected from the team member giving you a, "No," answer, you are in the unhealthy, territorial category. If you see opportunity through their "No," answer, you are in the healthy leader category.

What is team?

I love team. That should be a bumper sticker! The team style of leadership is inspirational. Team means going to those heights together, dreaming together and depending on one another to rise to those heights based on relationship and fueled by our gifts and talents blending together. It takes an ExO leader to make a team.

What does "team" mean to you? Is it a place where innovation can thrive? Is it one way you can change the world one leader at a time? There are many ways to build a team, but I believe the first way needs to be humility.

Without trust, there is nothing to build on. Trust brings everything together and allows your team to go to unseen heights together. It takes a good and healthy leader to build a strong and healthy team. When a leader knows and understands his place on the team, it becomes a fun and thriving organization. People will be begging to be on your team. This is not meant to boost your ego, but to be an example of what you're doing right.

A leader is not meant to say, "Jump" and everyone else says, "How high, your majesty?" That is anti-team. It causes people to bend under pressure, burn out and break. That is the main cause of companies imploding, churches crumbling and businesses not retaining good help. If we, as leaders, would look at who we *really* are, and not try to hide it, since it's not really hidden anyway, organizations would reach the heights they were intended for.

It is tragic when that lone voice in the crowd reaches a breaking point we just talked about. *As a leader, we have a responsibility to hear what those under us are saying.* It is our job to listen with an open mind, even if it is painful and will require change. That lone voice gets tired of being verbally bashed because he speaks up for truth and reality. He will reach the anger breaking point and his body will react, much like Mack's did in Dr. Seuss's story. Mack burped. It's a natural and normal thing when our bodies react because of the pressure we are under. Ulcers come, rashes appear, blood pressure goes up, and unusual heart rhythms materialize.

One day, unhealthy leaders will be thrown down from their high towers by their very own doing and be able to see reality as it really is. They won't be shouting orders from the sky, but picking mud out of their eyes like a turtle being thrown down into his pond. This would be a beginning point. Unhealthy leaders can learn from their mistakes and change, or they can retaliate and go after the lone voice for "burping."

When unhealthy leaders put themselves in a self-proclaimed successful position they are, in essence, building the company, the organization or the church on their personality and their abilities. If it's built on you alone, when you're gone, it will collapse. As a leader you are replaceable. You won't be the top dog forever. If leaders could just grasp that, they could more easily lead others to greatness. But it's hard to lead with a burden on your back. You see, when leaders carry the entire burden of the vision by themselves, they build up pressure that no one is equipped to handle. If the vision is birthed, carried, and implemented by the team, the organization will be sustained as leaders come and go. When it's built on a vision and not a person, then health and strength will last through the test of time. When you, as the leader, are no longer at the helm, your ideals will be carried on through the fingerprints you've left behind as you made impressions on the lives of people you impacted, poured into and focused on.

Leaders carry a lot on their shoulders. It's a gift to be a leader, but unhealthy leaders turn this gift into a curse by not giving up parts of the burden. So why are you a leader? Is it for financial gain, or maybe the perks? Maybe you are a leader to pass on what you've learned and take in what others can teach you as well. Are you leading in an "on purpose" way? Meaning, are you leading with intention? An ExO leader looks for ways to guide, mentor and learn.

What it takes to be a team leader

Think about this: What will be said about you at your funeral? Will your employees or staff attend out of obligation, or will they truly have been impacted and changed by your influence in their life? Your funeral will tell a lot about how you lived your life. Of course, by then it's too late to make changes. What's done is done. Remember the Charles Dickens story of Scrooge? In one of his dreams, he was so disliked that his sheets were taken off his bed while they were still warm. I'm just assuming here, but if there was a funeral for Scrooge, chances are no one would have shown up. He was truly in business for himself.

Scrooge had the opportunity to change how he would lead. He became a true team leader, and healthy in his relationships. He saw the value of team and chose to be accountable and vulnerable with his team. He led in truth, openness and honesty, putting away pride, his threatened heart and his arrogance. This can be very difficult for an unhealthy leader.

If unhealthy leaders capitalize on a second chance and truly change, not only will they be free from their unhealthy leadership style, but so will the employees and staff members around them. They can then help other leaders learn from their mistakes, freeing more staff members in their organization.

Being a healthy, ExO leader can be described as someone who doesn't want to shine, but wants to pass on principles and values necessary to being a healthy leader, enabling others to shine They are more interested in people than they are in their name being on the letterhead by keeping the focus on the principles and not on their personality. This is the beginning of a healthy influential leader that others will not only follow, but also commit to. A leader cannot lead unless he has a following. That following is a group of people whom the leader cannot do without. That following is the key to the success of the organization. Independent leaders are not leaders at all. An ExO leader takes others with him. He shows them the way and teaches them what he's learned. Let's continue on the topic of what an ExO, or a healthy leader, really looks like in the next section.

"A great man is always willing to be little."

Ralph Waldo Emerson

ExO 4
Team Building

Team building can only happen by people working together with respect at the core. The athletic department of the United States Military Academy has five core beliefs to build their sports teams on.

1. Respect

Respect is treating people the way they should be treated. If you are respectful, you recognize the dignity and worth of all individuals and honor their beliefs, customs, and heritage. Those associated with sports show respect by treating themselves, other persons, institutions, and their sport according to the highest standards of conduct.

2. Responsibility

Responsibility implies dependability and reliability. When you are responsible, all team members can count on you. You work hard to improve and have the perseverance to get through difficult times. You are committed to excellence and do everything within your power to complete the mission of the team. Cadets demonstrate responsibility by making progress toward becoming a leader of character their top priority. They hold themselves accountable for their actions and their decisions. They solve problems rather than make excuses and are reliable team members.

3. Integrity

Integrity is the cornerstone of good character and encompasses every part of your life. If you have integrity, your words are free from deceit and your actions are consistent with your words. You know what you stand for, and you live by the standards that you set. Integrity means keeping commitments and conducting honest behavior.

4. Servant leadership

Servant leadership refers to putting the team first and becoming responsible for personal and group roles while performing at your best. Cadets have a primary purpose of serving others while striving to become a personal and team leader.

5. Sportsmanship

Sportsmanship is the cooperation of cadets as a unit showing common courtesy, patience, pride, and respect. The conduct of DPE Competitive Sports according to the highest standards is our expectation for sportsmanship. Sport educators, CICs, coaches, officials, players, and spectators are expected to act correctly and demonstrate fairness and equity in all contests and relationships.

These five core values are principles that their sports teams hold to. If the coaches don't hold to them, then the teams will become chaotic and fall apart. If the participants, in this case the cadets, don't hold to them the coaches will be frustrated and the team will have a hard time winning. Team building is absolutely necessary to maintain a healthy team. These core values are not for the players only. They also expect the coaches to function this way.

Bruce E Brown, NAIA special presenter, gives what he calls, "The Difference between Good Coaches and Great Coaches."

Good coaches are positive – Great coaches have a positive passion.

Good coaches have strong beliefs – Great coaches are believed.

Good coaches understand the game – Great coaches understand the game and their athletes and how to teach both.

Good coaches talk about their expectations – Great coaches have athletes who meet their expectations.

Between each of those statements is a space, or a gap if you will. That is called the place of decision. It is here where a leader makes the decision to either stay the same (which would ultimately be to return to the same pattern), or to make some changes and become a great leader.

There are not only athletic departments and small businesses that work in this manner, but large corporations whose focus is also team building. In doing some research, I have chosen to show you three of them. I have quoted each of these three companies' mottos from their "career" page on their websites. Please note that I am not endorsing these companies or the causes they stand for. The only purpose for presenting these quotes is to bring your attention to team building.

1. *"GE is a place where you can live your dreams. Our global presence, innovation and financial strength help to make GE a dynamic place to work, giving you the advantage of a large company, with the agility of a small company, where your voice is heard."*
www.gecareers.com.

I like this quote because first of all, it not only says the company is important, but they have included the employee. How many companies will actually say that your voice, at the bottom of the stack, is important enough to be heard in a global corporation? I have never worked at GE, nor have I known anyone who has been an employee there, so I cannot confirm if this statement is played out in their day to day operations. But let's gather the healthy statements and apply them to our day to day operations. This quote gives me the sense that the company is big enough for me to grow into, to be able to dream, and a place where they will listen to my dreams.

2. *"Caterpillar leadership stems from its strong career development programs, flourishing worldwide presence, and unmatched technological expertise. But truth be told, our values—integrity, excellence, teamwork and commitment—are what guide us everywhere we operate. Our values set us apart as corporate citizens and as individuals. And they are the cornerstones of our business success."* www.cat.com.

This quote from Caterpillar is very similar to GE in its language. They are global, but yet embrace values that drive their success. They appear to use those values as a guide, or in their language, using them as a "cornerstone" for their success. If the top leadership does not keep these values then this company would not last; it would implode. If they use these values as a "cornerstone," then implosion is not likely to ever be their demise. These values make for a very solid company or corporation by providing goals for each and every employee, no matter which rung of the ladder they are standing on. If this is not held up by the executive leadership, those working beside or below them would not have a point of reference to take to the table and hold the company accountable to their own words. This is a healthy motto that everyone within this company can live up to.

3. *"Drive. Dedication. A passion for exceptional performance and service. These are the qualities that have built Lowe's into a dynamic and respected industry leader. Our 205,000+ employees share this unique spirit - with each other and with our customers every single day. If you have what it takes to help us keep building our story of success, we invite you to learn more about an amazing career with Lowe's."* www.lowes.com.

When I first read this motto from Lowe's, I was a little frustrated with the last part that says, "if you have what it takes to help us…" In and of itself, it sounds very company-centered, as though when you join their workforce you no longer matter as an individual. But in researching other areas, I have come to realize that they expand this motto in language such as, *"treating customers, co-workers, communities, investors, and vendors with respect and dignity in all interactions."*

They also say this: *"The secret to our success is our exceptional people. That's why we work hard to make sure that every Lowe's employee has the tools and training they need to build a rewarding career and promising future with our company. Lowe's is dedicated to helping our employees maximize their existing skills, and develop new talents and leadership abilities, through specialized programs."*

So once again the language appears to be that if you work on our team, we will assist you in growth. As you assist us in growing the company, we will help you grow. This is much different from the leader or company who wants to hire you for their benefit. They will benefit from you as they also train you. Our last company is The Home Depot.

Diversity is the catalyst for innovative thinking, entrepreneurial spirit and new ways of building our communities. The greater the diversity of our people, the greater our ability to serve our customers. At The Home Depot, we firmly believe that talent comes in many forms, and we celebrate each and every one of them. It is talent above all else that is cultivated, nourished and is considered to be the foundation of our culture.

We realize that as we continue to grow locally and globally, we will increasingly need all of our associates to continue contributing their best efforts. At The Home Depot, we are committed to creating a diverse work environment where all associates are included, respected and supported to do their best work. With pride, we recognize the uniqueness of each associate and the benefits of developing all associates to reach their full potential. With passion, we strive to promote a workplace where all associates have the opportunity to learn, grow and contribute. And with the united efforts of our people, we continue to provide superior value and service to all customers. That's why we say The Home Depot is one team, many talents. Celebrating diversity, practicing inclusion." www.homedepot.com.

Did you catch the statement, "*The greater the diversity of our people, the greater our ability to serve our customers."* What this says to me is they don't want clones. They aren't interested in everyone thinking the same. This has nothing to do with the code of conduct policies or the uniforms that are required. Instead, this has everything to do with what a person brings to the table through their innovative ideas. Some organizations are offering their employees a suggestion card where they can share their ideas. The upper level leaders of a company aren't out on the floor, making them to some degree, sheltered from the reality of what's really going on. Suggestion cards help eliminate some of the non-reality leading. It's hard to take a company in a direction without knowing the real concerns of its employees.

The same is true in a church ministry. The pastor would have a difficult time taking his staff, and eventually the entire church in a specific direction if he, as the main leader, is not aware of the needs of the church. He must lean on his staff for those answers, as well as the comment cards that are frequently put into the offering plate. A pastor should take those suggestions seriously and contemplate them with his core staff.

The next statement from The Home Depot that is worth noting is, "*…we firmly believe that talent comes in many forms, and we celebrate each and every one of them. It is talent above all else that is cultivated, nourished* *and is considered to be the foundation of our culture".*

The foundation of our culture is innovation. America was built on innovation. Being innovative does not mean being a natural born leader, but an innovationist needs a leader to nurture that talent. An organization with this statement should be strong in staff or employee development.

The point we can take from this quote is that someone, somewhere needs to be the leader who sets the tone for the organization by noticing the talents of those who work for them. The core leadership should also be trained to do this. In time, your organization will be known as one that discovers and develops new leaders. The amazing part is those who are developed will not only work to strengthen your organization, but they will also move to other organizations, and grow them by continuing the model you started in them. They will look for talent in others and continue that pattern of leadership. That is how The Home Depot's vision statement can include; *"We recognize the uniqueness of each associate* and *the benefits of developing all associates to reach their full potential."* That is the "discover and develop" way of leading.

When an organization has an assertive, healthy leader who understands who they are as a leader, but also takes it to the next level and passes that on to the core leaders around him, and they pass it on to those in their area, there are no limits to the success of this company and those who work there. When a leader allows for "diversity" but "practices inclusion" as The Home Depot put it, this allows for input from many sources, but allows the upper leadership to make the final call. When employees or staff feel like they have a stake in the organization, they will put forth much more of their effort. Being heard is a reward, but being heard *and* valued is much different.

Allow me to explain. Being heard is when the leader, or the boss listens to your concerns, nods his head and says; "Well I can see that you feel very passionately about this matter. I hope that having talked about it with me has helped." But being heard *and* valued is when the boss says; "Well I can see that you feel very passionately about this matter, which has caused you to come see me today. What do you think should be done about it?" At this juncture, he takes notes from *your* suggestions! He ends the conversation by saying, "I appreciate your work and the effort you are putting into this organization. It would not be what it is without your concern and ideas. Your input is vital to the success of this company."

It's not just about the language used, which is extremely vital, but it's the truth behind it. Do you, as the leader, mean what you are saying, or are they just empty words? No one likes a fake leader. No one likes an organization that promises big things but never delivers. Don't pretend to be a leader that you really aren't. Don't make your organization out to be something it isn't. Both will be found out and the results of that are negative for you as the leader and for the integrity of your organization. Being a team leader is rewarding. *But being a team builder is extraordinary.* It takes more than just having read the latest book on leadership to be a team builder. It takes perception to look into other people's lives and realize the talents that are surfacing. It takes willingness to help excavate that talent and assist that person in building it. That's how you build a team. It takes a leader who's assertive and truly desires others to succeed. This kind of ExO leader can be hard to find.

The non-assertive leader

I've brought out the attributes of a team leader, as well as the benefits to the team as the leader captures this leadership style. But it would be unbalanced to not also surface the non-assertive type of leader. At the outset, it doesn't sound so bad to be this type of leader. It has the feel of "laid back" and "relaxed." While it is true that to be a healthy leader, one needs to have those type of qualities and not just function in the fast forward mode all of the time, it is also true that if a leader shows no assertion towards meeting the goal, or building a relationship with those he works with, he is at risk of being unhealthy and creating unbalance in the team. Let's take a few moments and define who this leader is.

The non-assertive leader can tend to be complex. Sometimes he is a forward thinker and sometimes he is not. He sometimes doesn't mind when things stay the same and is satisfied with "good" having little interest in being "great." Non-assertive doesn't mean a leader who doesn't care. This leader cares about the organization, but he doesn't know how to handle a team. The non-assertive leader doesn't spend much time team building, since all his assertions are spent on the projects he needs to get done. He is task-oriented. There is a difference in task-oriented and detail-oriented. The non-assertive leader oftentimes misses many details since his goal is to finish a task. This frustrates a team since they are depending on him to do his part.

A non-assertive leader is someone who isn't power hungry. He is a quiet leader who doesn't speak up much, doesn't demand, and in all reality, he doesn't lead. He loves people, but communication is not his speciality. His style of leading allows others to tell him how to lead. He rarely takes the initiative to change or reach new heights for himself. In relation to his team, he leads from crisis to crisis. This happens because he does not notice behaviors or signals from his team. He is a non-observant person. Not just in his job, but in life as a whole. Eventually, team members will be frustrated with this type of leadership. In vocalizing their frustration, he will then allow the crisis to jolt him into a stage of seeking out his unhealthy leadership style. In time, this same scenario will happen all over again and again, and again. Eventually, this team member will come to a point of complete frustration causing him to give up and quit. Of course this will cause the non-assertive leader concern. But in the end, the question will be: Is it going to help him change how he leads, or will his pattern continue?

Being a non-assertive leader also means he will ignore disunity that needs resolving, tough decisions need to be made, and new vision that needs to be cast. The non-assertive leader cannot move towards the decision, but chooses to move away from it, or to pass it on to others who are willing to take the lead. In time, the staff under this leader will face frustration. It won't take long and the staff will begin jockeying for position. Someone needs to be the leader. If the leader isn't going to lead, then someone will. This frustration grows and begins to infect every aspect of the organization, spreading like a fast growing cancer, infecting every member it touches. The end result can be someone on the team demanding the position of authority. At this point, chances are high that this demanding team member has crawled over others around him to get this position, crushing any team unity, resulting in a very lonely corner office and not many friends. The non-assertive leader lets the team tell him what to do, instead of being the one who casts vision and guides the team to a positive and unified decision. This is because he battles low self-esteem. He doesn't want to sound demanding and would rather be everyone's buddy. He is not in relationship with his team to the point of impact because of his fear of failure. Surface relationships are not impacting, or life changing. This leader tends to get wrapped up in doing tasks right, but for the wrong reason. Because he fears failure, his focus is not to accomplish tasks out of relationship, which would be disappointing to his team. As long as he is not relational, he will continue to stay in this vicious cycle.

Because of this, the non-assertive leader oftentimes leads solo, which does not allow for accountability. It's not that he is against it, but the non-assertive leader isn't relationship driven. He does not see the need, resulting in frustration in his team, and in himself. What happens when a leader functions in this way, is he will forget important matters, that he, as the leader, is responsible for. He tries to get his job done right, but he keeps failing. His team will begin to fall apart because they have been the ones to hold him accountable, which is not entirely their responsibility. Because of the way the non-assertive leader leads, unhealthy traits are brought to the team. At some point, he will either change and become a successful team leader, or he will fail and need to find an occupation of which he is not the leader.

The difficult situation for this organization will be dealing with broken trust. Because the non-assertive leader could not be depended on, his team lost trust in his ability to keep cohesion in the team. No one wants to be on a team when there isn't a leader. If there is not a healthy leader giving a vision, followed with the necessary attributes to assist in helping the team make and reach goals to fulfill this vision, his team will cease to stand by his side. Instead, they will shift their loyalty to the one on the team who is a stronger leader. This is difficult for the entire organization.

But even more difficult will be this new leader, having overthrown the non-assertive leader, not being able to gain any type of support of the whole team. Sure there would be some who get on his team. But as for unity in the entire team, if it comes at all, will come only through humility. This new leader who spoke loudly and thought he knew how to do it right, is now facing a disassembled team who isn't going to naturally be on his team just because he can speak louder than the last guy.

Non-assertive leaders run the risk of allowing this type of unhealthy behavior to rear it's ugly head and dismantle, or possibly destroy, an entire organization, all because he was afraid to speak up. This leader can be easily walked all over, causing this fallout to happen.

What causes a leader to have such a lack of confidence? It should seem obvious to him that if he isn't the one who keeps it together from the top down, someone, somewhere will try to overthrow him. But a non-aggressive leader runs from conflict. He runs from personal opinions. He feels safer in his office, away from people, just quietly doing his job. The reality is, he isn't doing his job. Pushing papers is not his only job. A leader has a responsibility to create more opportunity for his staff and employees to grow, be trained and have the availability to be heard.

This does not mean a non-assertive leader cannot become a healthy leader. It will take confidence and training. When a non-assertive leader decides to change, it is vital that he has a coach to help him make and meet new goals. Goals are different than deadlines. To meet a deadline all you have to do is get the work done. To meet a goal, you oftentimes have to change. This is where the non-assertive leader struggles. He has been very faithful at meeting his deadlines, but has not had many personal goals to reach. It will take small goals and steps to begin bringing this leader to a place of confidence.

To wrap up this section, allow me to unpack a style of leading that includes being both assertive and non-assertive.

A leader who balances his leadership by knowing when to be assertive and when not to be is an ExO leader indeed! There are some leaders who appear to be vague, or non-assertive, but do not feel vague on the inside. Example: A leader is interviewed for a position and is asked specific questions concerning vision for the company or organization. This leader gives what appears to be a humble answer by saying, "I don't know," meaning he will let time reveal the answer and let vision unfold. But in time, this leader will either have an answer to the "I don't know" questions, or he will continue to say "I don't know." He really does know how to lead, but isn't saying that in order to manipulate others. This is a subtle and damaging way to lead.

So let me clear up this confusing leadership style. If a leader wants to lead an organization or a team of people, he should have an idea of where he's going. It is possible for a healthy leader to say, "I don't know," but with the goal of allowing the team to help organize and create the vision. That is healthy and beneficial. He may not know exactly what the path looks like, but if he is gifted to lead, there is some level of vision that must be released. It helps a team to have a leader who can chart a path, even without all the details in place. Some form of assertiveness is vital to the morale of a team.

Which leader are you most likely to resemble? Honest evaluation is necessary to being the best and most healthy leader you can be. Asking your core staff to fill out an evaluation form critiquing your leadership is necessary in seeking out a well-rounded view of how you lead. Ask questions that are relevant to your line of work. Asking questions that pertain directly to your place of leadership will let those evaluating you know that you want specific answers. But let me give you a simple warning. If you proceed with an evaluation, it is vital that those who fill out the evaluation feel protected from any retaliation on your part. If they feel at all threatened by you, assuming that what they say will cause a back draft and will be reprimanded for their comments, then you might want to deal with your own insecurities, or find a new job that does not include being a leader, but a follower instead so you can identify with their role. You will read comments you won't like. You might even lose sleep over it. Wrestling over it is healthy in the fact that you are wrestling with who others perceive you to be. These are people who work determine to allow their evaluation of you to shape reality, then you are on your way to becoming a healthier leader. If you do not and choose to hear the good and ignore the bad comments, you are surfacing unhealthy leadership, making that evaluation more important than you might think. You are not going to please everyone, nor should you. Your goal should be to move toward health, making your team's evaluation vital to your forward motion.

On this note, I would like to share with you some comments made by a proven ExO leader indeed. Read on to hear more about healthy leadership.

"Pride is concerned with who is right. Humility is concerned with what is right."

Ezra Taft Benson

ExO 5
Words From ExO Leaders

Words From A Known Leader

Colin Powell is known for his leadership as a General in the U.S. Army, Secretary of State, our National Security Advisor, among other positions. It is appropriate for us to take a few lessons from his leadership tips given in a recorded interview with Bill Hybels from a Willow Creek Leadership Summit. His beliefs about what makes a good leader will help us understand what a healthy leader looks like. Here are some of those lessons with my comments to follow: (For the complete listing of this article, go to: http://blog.buildingchurchleaders.com/2008/03/colin_powell_15_tips_on_leader.html.)

1. Leadership should promote a clash of ideas. This is called a "noisy system".

Have you ever been in a planning meeting with your boss where he did all the talking? On the other hand have you ever been in the same type of meeting allowing you to freely share your ideas and even allow you to disagree with his plan of action and not fire you? That is a noisy system. It is when openness is not only welcomed, but disagreement is appreciated. It is difficult to progress forward when everyone agrees with everything you say. A noisy system is a controlled environment where all participants can safely share their opinions. Ideas are the voice of the heart and a reflection of the soul. When people bring their ideas to the table, they are laying down their heart. What are you, the leader, going to do with their heart? In the same regard, when ideas are expressed, assist in the possible clash. Make some clear boundaries as to what is allowed in your noisy system and what is not appropriate. It is easy for chaos to appear within noise, making it ripe for emotions to take over and people to get hurt. Promote the clash, but provide the boundaries.

2. Plans don't accomplish anything – people do.

There is nothing more frustrating than being involved with a group of leaders and nobody leads. The meetings are nothing more than people sharing ideas. Without a plan of action, their voices change nothing, their leadership does not affect the world, and they didn't accomplish anything. A strategy is needed. Everyone on your team brings a particular "flavor." If you don't know what those flavors are, ask them what they bring to the team in the way of their talents. One might like organizing, one hate it. Don't give the one who hates organizing the task of organizing the next customer service training. Maybe they are a great teacher. Then they are the ones who should do the teaching at the training sessions, but someone else should set it up. You can make all the plans you want, but if you don't have the right people to implement them, you are wasting your time and the talents of your team members.

3. If you have an issue, come see me.

The open door policy is a much-needed policy in the office sector. When a subordinate has a concern or a question that needs attention from the top, they need to feel free to express that. This will bring better productivity and produce better results on a professional level. It will also provide a better working environment so all employees have an open door to express their feelings and thoughts knowing they will not be turned away, fired or rejected. They will not take the issue to others, creating what could be a hostile situation, breeding contempt with the other employees. Having an open door policy will create ease in the workplace. It will encourage less stress and more freedom enabling them to connect with you and the other employees. These moments are perfect for mentoring and leadership training. One thing is for sure – there will be conflict in the workplace. People are human. Everyone has different concerns and opinions. The question is: How will you handle that? Have you provided a safe environment for your staff members to approach you? Will you assist them in resolving their conflict, and capitalize on the opportunity to mentor them in conflict resolution? This could be a grand opportunity for this staff member to share with you some new and innovative ideas that may resolve the issue. You don't need to have all the answers. They just might hold the answer and in coming to you, have the opportunity to share it. Don't be so wrapped up in your position that you miss these moments. Provide an opportunity for everyone on your team to learn and grow in their leadership abilities.

4. Probe the organization.

This is very closely linked to number three because when you go to the boss, he can either take what you say at face value, or go through the chain of command, evaluating if it is an individual or team issue. This is a decision for a boss to make. Because it not only holds the initial person with the argument responsible for what he says, but sends a message to the entire company that the boss is not afraid of conflict. He will do what needs to be done to better the workplace and is bold enough to address the things that need to be adjusted in the organization. Remember: an organization is built on people, not one person. If it's built on you this probe won't happen. The very word probe means to explore. No "one" person wants to be explored. If an entire organization is going to become stronger, it will need probing and undergo scrutiny. It must be done above the table, safely and with the betterment of the organization and it's employees in mind.

5. Reward your best performers; get rid of the worst ones.

This might seem harsh, but if you have an employee who is what we might call "lethargic", that attitude will eventually spread to the whole workplace. He is a vision sucker. People who bring little productivity to work also affect the productivity of others, making it harder for the goals of the vision to be met, frustrating the entire group. For a company to be healthy, to grow and expand, it needs a team of people with the same common goal. If some "players" on the team don't really care about making a touchdown, it would be better they get out of the game and find the appropriate sport for them. The biggest caution with this is the process. There is a right way and a wrong way. The wrong way is to make a person feel unproductive, rejected and worthless. The right way is to acknowledge their gifts and talents and assist them in acquiring a suitable place of involvement where they would best be used. Maybe they can be moved to another department and flourish there. Maybe it will be a complete transition to another workplace. It is possible they were ready to move on but didn't know how to articulate that to you. The point is, there are times when people need to either move or be moved to a better situation for the benefit of the company or for themselves, or both. It should be a decision that will help them feel like the move is a "win" for them. They should not feel they are getting the short end of the stick. This is considering they are not being asked to move based on illegal or malicious behavior. If that were the case, they would need to move on.

6. Be prepared to disappoint people.

There will come a time when the leader has to make decisions based on all the opinions given. The leader has to be responsible to say "no" to some, while saying, "yes" to others, for the good of the company or organization. Not everyone is going to like you. But more will respect you for keeping the vision than those who will be disgruntled that you didn't agree with their desires. These type of people are like little kings running around in circles. They don't have a crown, but want one. They don't have the influence they think they deserve so they pretend to have it by putting demands on the boss. The boss has to be able to see through this facade and either help them realize their place, or allow them to move on.

7. Check your ego at the door.

This falls in line with number six. It is vital to a team to understand that when you allow open discussion on particular topics, some people are not open handed with their words; they have their feelings attached to the sleeve of that hand. They are what we can call territorial. Their words reflect their heart and if you do not accept what they say, they feel rejected. This is why it's important to discuss this openly in team meetings. Do a series of teaching, training or mentoring on the topic of territorialism. Have a questionnaire for them to fill out after a teaching and review it with them privately. In order for them to know what it means to check their ego at the door, they will need to see you, the ExO leader, do it first. Don't flex your muscles and then try to mentor on how to let your ego go. Don't be brash and then teach on servanthood. Nobody likes a hypocrite.

8. Have fun along the way.

Being the leader is not always fun, but it can be. You don't need to make more money so you can buy all the big boy toys and hit the lake and the hills every weekend with your fancy gear. It means you can be fun at the office too. A boss who is serious day in and day out tends to be a workaholic and demands everyone else be one too. Take the office staff out for lunch once a month and let the company foot the bill. Have a fun party around the holidays. Remember birthdays. Do things that will let your staff know you care and want to be part of their lives. Be human. When is the last time your staff has seen you laugh? Do you have anything funny in your office? Maybe a funny cartoon clip, or a comical, non-offensive plaque or sign would be a nice touch, right beside the "Boss of the Year" award. If you just felt offended by that, may I say that a plaque given to you by people who don't work side by side with you, and look only at numbers, shouldn't be as valuable to you as the loyalty of the people around you. Are you so driven that you can't notice the woman at the desk who is coughing from bronchitis? Or how about the man down the hall who just lost his wife to cancer? Sensitive leaders are available leaders. They are available to notice others. On the same token, fun leaders are respected and seen as human, and tend to treat others with respect. If you are an up-tight leader, take a moment and consider how you make the office a fun place for everyone. Maybe even those who are hurting can find a place of comfort on your watch.

9. Cast no stereotypes.

Evaluate people on their performance only. If the color of their skin bothers you, buy an island and live with the penguins. Well, then again, maybe not...they are black *and* white. The bottom line is this: evaluate people only on their work. Appreciate them for their humanity and choose to be colorblind. Besides skin color, personality hang-ups can be a major roadblock. An ExO leader does not shun those who are different from themselves, but welcomes differing opinions, backgrounds and educations. In the same context, an ExO leader encourages the quiet team members to speak up and be heard. You never know if they have the next winning idea for the company! Quiet people tend to listen and watch, surmising more than you think. An ExO leader also knows how to help the one who frequently speaks up and dominates the staff meetings. To be a healthy leader, it's vital to recognize the various types of personalities and flavor that each person brings to your round table. If you are quick to cast a stereotype, it could be that you are cutting out the very person that has an idea that will take your company to its next level. Capitalize on your team and it's diversity!

10. Perpetual optimism is a force multiplier.

Think of it this way: when the leader is a strong believer in the decision at hand, he must remain optimistic about its success. As he continues to voice this message, it will begin to multiply with others over and over putting optimistic force behind the decision. If the leader is walking in constant worry over the state of the vision, the team will fall right in line and pessimism will dominate every decision made. An ExO leader will help keep the vision higher than the clouds. He will do what he can to keep chins off the ground and constantly stir the pot of optimism and innovation. When that happens, the staff is fully connected to the direction the organization is headed and will follow. That optimism is a force that will carry over into the decisions, which leads into the next point...

11. Trust is the key.

When you, the leader, allow your staff into your world, they will trust you more. For example, if you just carry out your regular duties as the "big guy" in the big office, they will distance themselves from you, never getting to know the real you. It's hard to trust someone you don't know. When the force of optimism is in place, trust is at an all time high. When the leader knows that, he can keep the trust and make the right decisions based on the team's goals and the vision at hand, or he can manipulate the team to get what he wants. Manipulating will obviously break trust and the force of any kind is lost. If you want to be a successful leader, build trust and build it often. Choose to do things that will build trust on purpose. Leading with intention is vital to being an ExO leader. In our day and age, we wonder who we can trust. So many who have climbed the ladder of success have fallen and hit every rung on the ladder as they have descended down. Your "people" will know if they can trust you. I live like this: I trust people until they give me a reason not to." I haven't always lived like this, but over time, I have been able to judge character more quickly. My hope is that this book will help you do the same. But I also would like you to be the one building trust in those who work for you and with you. Trust will build a lot of bridges, just as distrust blows them up. The only way to cross the bridge is through trust. Use the material you're given, and start building!

12. Avoid war if at all possible.

Evaluate the cost of the battle. Often those with leadership gifts are passionate and outspoken people. They can be opinionated and like to often share those opinions. War is something that energizes this kind of leader because it's a good excuse to talk loudly! But to be a trustworthy leader, it's important to determine what it means to go to war over an issue or a topic in your workplace. Is it a core value that is being challenged? If it is, it should be discussed at length. This is called diplomacy. Sit down with your staff and allow the varying opinions to be heard. Once again, a good leader allows for conflict, but doesn't get wrapped up in it. Remember, leave the ego at the door and don't let your personality conflict with your professional views. They are going to be linked, but if you let your personality influence the show, a war is well underway and people will get hurt from the shrapnel of words from around the table. Work out the disagreements, even if they are fundamental differences. Where there's a will there's a way. If you prefer a war which you and your opinions can win, that's exactly what you'll get and experience many casualties. Avoiding war is not the same as avoiding conflict. It simply means to enter into diplomatic talks and allow opinions to be heard and issues to be considered.

From those twelve points and all the other ideas given, one should be able to lead the healthy way. That's what this book is all about: helping you see the difference between healthy and unhealthy leading, allowing you to become an ExO leader. The next and final step in this book is helping the one who has been under the authority of an unhealthy leader.

Words From An Unknown Leader

It may seem impossible to follow the example of Colin Powell's leadership. So to balance that out, I felt you needed to hear a few words from an unlikely source: a janitor. This story is written by Col. James Moschgat, 12th Operations Group Commander, Graduate United States Air Force Academy - class of 1977.

"William "Bill" Crawford certainly was an unimpressive figure, one you could easily overlook during a hectic day at the U.S. Air Force Academy. Mr. Crawford, as most of us referred to him back in the late 1970s, was our squadron janitor.

While we cadets busied ourselves preparing for academic exams, athletic events, Saturday morning parades and room inspections, or never-ending leadership classes, Bill quietly moved about the squadron mopping and buffing floors, emptying trash cans, cleaning toilets, or just tidying up the mess 100 college-age kids can leave in a dormitory.

Sadly, and for many years, few of us gave him much notice, rendering little more than a passing nod or throwing a curt, "G'morning!" in his direction as we hurried off to our daily duties. Why? Perhaps it was because of the way he did his job-he always kept the squadron area spotlessly clean, even the toilets and showers gleamed. Frankly, he did his job so well, none of us had to notice or get involved. After all, cleaning toilets was his job, not ours.

Maybe it was his physical appearance that made him disappear into the background. Bill didn't move very quickly and, in fact, you could say he even shuffled a bit, as if he suffered from some sort of injury. His gray hair and wrinkled face made him appear ancient to a group of young cadets. And his crooked smile, well, it looked a little funny.

Face it, Bill was an old man working in a young person's world. What did he have to offer us on a personal level?

Finally, maybe it was Mr. Crawford's personality that rendered him almost invisible to the young people around him. Bill was shy, almost painfully so. He seldom spoke to a cadet unless they addressed him first, and that didn't happen very often. Our janitor always buried himself in his work, moving about with stooped shoulders, a quiet gait, and an averted gaze. If he noticed the hustle and bustle of cadet life around him, it was hard to tell. So, for whatever reason, Bill blended into the woodwork and became just another fixture around the squadron. The Academy, one of our nation's premier leadership laboratories, kept us busy from dawn till dusk. And Mr. Crawford...well, he was just a janitor.

That changed one fall Saturday afternoon in 1976. I was reading a book about World War II and the tough Allied ground campaign in Italy, when I stumbled across an incredible story. On Sept. 13, 1943, a Private William Crawford from Colorado, assigned to the 36th Infantry Division, had been involved in some bloody fighting on Hill

424 near Altavilla, Italy. The words on the page leapt out at me: "in the face of intense and overwhelming hostile fire ... with no regard for personal safety on his own initiative, Private Crawford single-handedly attacked fortified enemy positions." It continued, "for conspicuous gallantry and intrepidity at risk of life above and beyond the call of duty, the President of the United States..." "Holy cow," I said to my roommate, "you're not going to believe this, but I think our janitor is a Medal of Honor winner."

We all knew Mr. Crawford was a WWII Army vet, but that didn't keep my friend from looking at me as if I was some sort of alien being. Nonetheless, we couldn't wait to ask Bill about the story on Monday. We met Mr. Crawford bright and early Monday and showed him the page in question from the book, anticipation and doubt on our faces.

He starred at it for a few silent moments and then quietly uttered something like, "Yep, that's me." Mouths agape, my roommate and I looked at one another, then at the book, and quickly back at our janitor. Almost at once we both stuttered, "Why didn't you ever tell us about it?" He slowly replied after some thought, "That was one day in my life and it happened a long time ago." I guess we were all at a loss for words after that. We had to hurry off to class and Bill, well he had chores to attend to.

However, after that brief exchange, things were never again the same around our squadron. Word spread like wildfire among the cadets that we had a hero in our midst - Mr. Crawford, our janitor, had won the Medal! Cadets who had once passed by Bill with hardly a glance, now greeted him with a smile and a respectful, "Good morning, Mr. Crawford."

Those who had before left a mess for the "janitor" to clean up started taking it upon themselves to put things in order. Most cadets routinely stopped to talk to Bill throughout the day and we even began inviting him to our formal squadron functions. He'd show up dressed in a conservative dark suit and quietly talk to those who approached him, the only sign of his heroics being a simple blue, star-spangled lapel pin.

Almost overnight, Bill went from being a simple fixture in our squadron to one of our teammates. Mr. Crawford changed too, but you had to look closely to notice the difference. After that fall day in 1976, he seemed to move with more purpose, his shoulders didn't seem to be as stooped, he met our greetings with a direct gaze and a stronger "good morning" in return, and he flashed his crooked smile more often. The squadron gleamed as always, but everyone now seemed to notice it more. Bill even got to know most of us by our first names, something that didn't happen often at the Academy.

While no one ever formally acknowledged the change, I think we became Bill's cadets and his squadron. As often happens in life, events sweep us away from those in our past. The last time I saw Bill was on graduation day in June 1977. As I walked out of the squadron for the last time, he shook my hand and simply said, "Good luck, young man."

With that, I embarked on a career that has been truly lucky and blessed. Mr. Crawford continued to work at the Academy and eventually retired in his native Colorado where he resides today, one of four Medal of Honor winners living in a small town.

A wise person once said, "It's not life that's important, but those you meet along the way that make the difference." Bill was one who made a difference for me. While I haven't seen Mr. Crawford in over twenty years, he'd probably be surprised to know I think of him often. Bill Crawford, our janitor, taught me many valuable, unforgettable leadership lessons. Here are ten I'd like to share with you.

1. Be Cautious of Labels. Labels you place on people may define your relationship to them and bound their potential. Sadly, and for a long time, we labeled Bill as just a janitor, but he was so much more. Therefore, be cautious of a leader who callously says, "Hey, he's just an Airman." Likewise, don't tolerate the O-1, who says, "I can't do that, I'm just a lieutenant."

2. Everyone Deserves Respect. Because we hung the "janitor" label on Mr. Crawford, we often wrongly treated him with less respect than others around us. He deserved much more, and not just because he was a Medal of Honor winner. Bill deserved respect because he was a janitor, walked among us, and was a part of our team.

3. Courtesy Makes a Difference. Be courteous to all around you, regardless of rank or position. Military customs, as well as common courtesies, help bond a team. When our daily words to Mr. Crawford turned from perfunctory "hellos" to heartfelt greetings, his demeanor and personality outwardly changed. It made a difference for all of us.

4. Take Time to Know Your People. Life in the military is hectic, but that's no excuse for not knowing the people you work for and with. For years a hero walked among us at the Academy and we never knew it. Who are the heroes that walk in your midst?

5. Anyone Can Be a Hero. Mr. Crawford certainly didn't fit anyone's standard definition of a hero. Moreover, he was just a private on the day he won his Medal. Don't sell your people short, for any one of them may be the hero who rises to the occasion when duty calls. On the

other hand, it's easy to turn to your proven performers when the chips are down, but don't ignore the rest of the team. Today's rookie could and should be tomorrow's superstar.

6. Leaders Should Be Humble. Most modern day heroes and some leaders are anything but humble, especially if you calibrate your "hero meter" on today's athletic fields. End zone celebrations and self-aggrandizement are what we've come to expect from sports greats. Not Mr. Crawford-he was too busy working to celebrate his past heroics. Leaders would be well served to do the same.

7. Life Won't Always Hand You What You Think You Deserve. We in the military work hard and, dang it, we deserve recognition, right? However, sometimes you just have to persevere, even when accolades don't come your way. Perhaps you weren't nominated for junior officer or airman of the quarter as you thought you should - don't let that stop you.

8. Don't pursue glory; pursue excellence. Private Bill Crawford didn't pursue glory; he did his duty and then swept floors for a living. No Job is Beneath a Leader. If Bill Crawford, a Medal of Honor winner, could clean latrines and smile, is there a job beneath your dignity? Think about it.

9. Pursue Excellences. No matter what task life hands you, do it well. Mr. Crawford modeled that philosophy and helped make our dormitory area a home.

10. Life is a Leadership Laboratory. All too often we look to some school or PME class to teach us about leadership when, in fact, life is a leadership laboratory. Those you meet everyday will teach you enduring lessons if you just take time to stop, look and listen. I spent four years at the Air Force Academy, took dozens of classes,

read hundreds of books, and met thousands of great people. I gleaned leadership skills from all of them, but one of the people I remember most is Mr. Bill Crawford and the lessons he unknowingly taught. Don't miss your opportunity to learn. Bill Crawford was a janitor. However, he was also a teacher, friend, role model and one great American hero. Thanks, Mr. Crawford, for some valuable leadership lessons.

And now, for the rest of the story.........Pvt. William John Crawford was a platoon scout for 3rd Platoon of Company L 142nd Regiment 36th Division (Texas National Guard) and won the Medal Of Honor for his actions on Hill 424, just 4 days after the invasion at Salerno. You can read his citation at: www.army.mil/cmh-pg/mohiia1.htm.

On Hill 424, Pvt. Crawford took out 3 enemy machine guns before darkness fell, halting the platoon's advance. Pvt. Crawford could not be found and was assumed dead. The request for his MOH was quickly approved. MG Terry Allen presented the posthumous MOH to Bill Crawford's father, George, on 11 May 1944 in Camp (now Fort) Carson, near Pueblo. Nearly two months after that, it was learned that Pvt. Crawford was alive in a POW camp in Germany. During his captivity, a German guard clubbed him with his rifle. Bill overpowered him, took the rifle away, and beat the guard unconscious. A German doctor's testimony saved him from severe punishment, perhaps death. To stay ahead of the advancing Russian army, the prisoners were marched 500 miles in 52 days in the middle of the German winter, subsisting on one potato a day. An allied tank column liberated the camp in the spring of 1945, and Pvt. Crawford took his first hot shower in 18 months on VE Day. Pvt. Crawford stayed in the army before retiring as a

MSG and becoming a janitor. You can read his story at: www.homeofheros.com/profiles.

    Not all leaders are sitting behind a desk. My boss, Matt, was behind a steering wheel as we commuted an hour, and then spent hours carrying a backpack vacuum, dusting a ten thousand dollar bureau, or making millionaires beds, doing laundry, and cleaning up dog hair. Maybe you don't need one more seminar. Maybe you just need to put your laptop to the side and listen to the conversation of those in your office. Maybe you need to put down your pen and your perception of leadership to reveal the heroes that are in your midst. You never know, they just might teach you a thing or two. Are you humble enough to handle that? Who will you be writing about in 20 years? Will you be looking back on your notes from all those great seminars you attended, or will you recall the simple lessons learned from just listening and noticing that one who was right under your nose. Maybe you'll write about a schoolteacher or your first boss as you worked on that ranch. Leaders are everywhere. But healthy leaders aren't. There are lessons to be learned around every corner. But to go around that corner, you will have to leave your office and get walking. So go, discover something new; discover someone you hadn't noticed before. And do me a favor – please write about it.

"Leadership is not magnetic personality, that can just as well be a glib tongue. It is not "making friends and influencing people", that is flattery. Leadership is lifting a person's vision to higher sights, the raising of a person's performance to a higher standard, the building of a personality beyond its normal limitations."

Peter F. Drucker

ExO 6
Healing

Have you worked for an unhealthy leader? If so, it takes some time to heal from the effects of this unhealthy leadership style. The first step in healing from this kind of experience is to quit thinking about it. Yes, that's the first step. You see, these kinds of painful experiences get into our mind like a rapid growing disease. It will consume your every thought, and eventually dominate your life and cause not only fatigue, but physical issues.

Burnout is a difficult thing to break out of because the source has been out of your control. But to conquer the effects of burnout, you need to stop thinking about it. Think about things that bring you happiness. As a Christian, I have gone to the Bible. Allow me to explain what you need to read and why.

Because this type of leader uses distorted power over you, it is vital that you renew your mind. You've had to succumb (means: die from the effect of a disease or injury) to his authority. Because this person was in authority over you, the decision to oppose what you were instructed to do was not in your hands, bringing on burnout. In other words, you were dying to what you felt to be right. "Maintaining" became your way of life – or rather, doing what you were expected to do, even though it went against your values. What happens then is, our minds begin to tolerate the circumstances in order to survive. But eventually we begin to melt down, as the situation gets too tense for us to handle.

While we are on the subject of leaders that use distorted power over others, it may be important to help paint the picture of what this really is, using the following scenario.

Let's say you are working for an unhealthy leader and the time for you to move on comes. You recognize you have other talents that have yet to be tapped into, and your current job will not help you develop those talents, so you move on. Your unhealthy boss doesn't want to release you, but you make your decision regardless of the consequences.

In time, you get a call from him. He wants you to come back and work for him. The problem is, you've found your niche and that niche doesn't include him or getting a check with his signature on it. You've discovered your calling and want to stick with it. But he keeps hounding you to come back and work for him. Why does he do that? Don't they care enough about you to see you have succeeded at what you were created to do? Well, not really. We are talking about a very selfish leader. He sees what will benefit him, not you. It's not about you, the little man on the bottom of the stack. It's all about your making this "king" look good and helping him get to the top so he can be king of it all.

Some of you may not like this comparison, but I must bring it to light. Hang on, this is going to offend some of you, make some of you uncomfortable and maybe even make some of you mad, but in all reality, we need to realize that at the heart of every human is a dark place that cries out for power and control. You may have worked for someone like this, or maybe you are or have been that person. I have done some research about pimps and prostitution at www.prostitutionresearch.com and have reviewed several facts, some of which I will highlight here as it relates to the unhealthy way of leading.

To me, this distorted way of life is the extreme of what we've been talking about in an unhealthy leader. It's the lowest form of leadership, but somehow, this leader feels it's the highest.

How does a pimp treat a prostitute? He owns her and uses her to bring in money for him to live high and mighty. He doesn't care about her life's calling. He selfishly uses her for his own gain, letting her "burn out." He likes the power and lords it over his prostitutes. A prostitute is not allowed to share about herself to "the johns," or to the customers. She is forced by the pimp to live in someone else's fantasy – someone else's vision for her life. She is not allowed to ruin that dream world or she could face a severe beating. She is being used to fulfill the fantasies of someone else – her dreams and value don't matter. That person is a legend in their own mind, not caring about anyone else but themselves.

There are leaders who do not allow their staff to share what they think, as this will lead to shattering the dream world that the leader is in. They will no longer be

able to build themselves up to see as far as they can, all by themselves. Their staff isn't there to share their mind, but to submit and fulfill the leaders dream. It's anti-team to lead this way. It's selfish and it destroys lives. There are some who have been the guy on the bottom of the stack who took the brunt of it all, sometimes taking a verbal beating for saying the wrong thing that would inevitably break the fantasy bubble this unhealthy leader lives in. This guy on the bottom of the stack is a prisoner and will eventually burn out, but not without deep wounds, much like a prostitute who is trapped in someone else's power, until she makes a break, which is very seldom.
With this extreme type of leadership exposed, let me remind you that there are many astounding leaders. We know some of them by name, and others have yet to be seen outside their small sphere of influence. Not every good leader is recognized in a book. There are plenty of good leaders around you. You may be one of them.

But to remain a healthy, ExO leader one must remain humble, teachable and willing to change. Without these components, the dark side in all of us will take us down a dangerous road. You will end up hurting people and ultimately hurting yourself. Leaders need to remember there is a dark side and it wants to take over.

This dark side is what makes leaders think they don't have to submit to anyone. It makes them proud and arrogant. It lies to them and tells them they are the "king" or "queen" and others are there to serve them. It preys on our egos, and it's very hungry for more attention and power. It is a daily choice to deny this hungry beast. It's not impossible, but it does take dedication and commitment to a bigger cause.

The bigger cause

It's not enough to wake up and say, "I'm going to be a good leader today." It takes one choosing, through his actions, to be a good leader. For example, someone in your office comes to you and says, "I loved what you did on that article. You are amazing." This presents a choice: either take the compliment as an encouragement, or take the compliment and let it feed the hungry beast of pride. A healthy, ExO leader takes that and says, "Thanks so much" and leaves it at that. But an unhealthy leader takes it and ponders it later, eventually believing the lie that they really are amazing, allowing this dark side called pride to begin to move in.

I believe that pride does go before a fall. When we let pride in, it brings darkness and we can't see the truth – we can't see where we're going and we will most certainly fall. Pride is like a mirage. It's not reality. When a leader moves into the power trip of feeling amazing they will eventually begin to want more attention that boosts this amazing feeling. If this attention is not deflected it will inflate pride and bring destruction. This moves a leader away from serving and into being served. As a leader, you need to choose which one you will live by. One of them will destroy you and one will give you freedom (not build you up). It seems ridiculous to constantly deny yourself, but when we as leaders do that, the message sent is worth it.

When leaders begin to move towards the thoughts that inflate their leadership ability instead of away from them, the slope gets very slippery. It is a battle to say "no" to what the dark side is demanding. It's a choice to not want what our flesh wants. When we as leaders choose to lead with humility, it becomes a lifestyle and the choosing isn't as hard. That's what it takes to become an ExO leader.

Territorial leaders

Territorial leaders have built an invisible wall around their ideas. They own and protect their ideas to the point of reinforcing them. If that wall is breached, what will come pouring out are some very nasty emotions and responses. Being territorial simply means putting their identity in their job, Jealousy rises up whenever someone threatens to take away any part of their identity. Unhealthy leaders prove their worth through their identity, making them territorial.

I believe God has given each person a calling. It's up to each individual to express their calling in a healthy way. I feel that my calling is to reach out to teenagers. I have used many resources to accomplish this. For instance, this book will be used to teach and train youth pastors and their volunteer staff. This book is one avenue that fulfills my calling. I believe that your calling fulfills you and your identity carries you. Since I am a Christian, that identity for me is in the identity of Jesus Christ. So since I have given my life to Jesus, I have taken on the task of changing things in my life so that my life looks like His life – His identity. I want to be like Jesus, so I purposely live my life in such a way that will reflect who Jesus of the Bible is. Since my identity is in Him, my job can't be my identity too. My calling can't even be my identity. I can live in total freedom as a leader by living this way. I am confident that God has given me tasks to do regarding my calling. Even if it's construction clean up and dusting the Italian furniture of millionaires mansions in Montana, I was able to learn something that benefited my calling. It may not have looked like it at first, but when it was all over, I saw the benefit of what I'd seen and done. When you allow circumstances that don't seem to fit, you will find in the end that there really was a purpose that benefited your calling.

No matter where you are, whether you're a young visionary, or a seasoned veteran, change is on the horizon. Things can't stay the same and stay healthy. It takes a humble leader to see the need for change. Humility is the pathway that will take you to greater vision. You could have a greater vision without humility, but it will lead you back to square one again and again. Pride is only a breath away. It's the breath that says, "Yeah, you're right. I am good." Pride reveals the weakness of a leader, which is most commonly insecurity. Insecurity becomes arrogance as a leader tries to rise above his insecurity through his authority instead of through humility. It won't take long and this type of leader will resort to lying in order to make himself out to be someone he is not. The sad reality is that he would be a good leader if he would stop trying to be someone he is not. As long as someone thinks he is the king of all he sees, then naturally he will do what it takes to see more and more.

So this leads us to the question: "Is it possible for a leader to be humble and confident at the same time?" You probably already know I'm going to say, "yes". If the leader's confidence is based on solid principles, a team code of ethics, knowledge and experience, confidence is sure to be there. With adequate boundaries, a leader can freely move, making it possible to lead with confidence. This builds confidence in this ExO leader, as well as those on the team. But there's more. As long as a leader remains team oriented, he cannot only lead with confidence, but with humility as he is allowing himself to be subject to the team. With that last statement, you may have just felt your heart leap. I did say that a confident and humble leader would need to be "subject to" the team. The leader is important, but not irreplaceable. Staying humble also includes realizing that as you raise up a team around you, any one of them could take your place, putting yourself in a lofty place is dangerous. After all, a team who feels threatened and challenged is in a place of defense. That simply means they can band together against you.

To lead with humility does not mean being a silent leader, but rather a leader who listens and respects another leaders views. It means that his ideas are not always the best, but the team knows that the final decision rests with him.

To lead with confidence, a leader knows where he is going and where he is taking the team, but he also realizes that he can't bully his way there. It will take time to sell the entire team on his goals and get them to join his mission. As he continues to lead this way, with humility and patience, the team's confidence in him will increase. A confident leader can sometimes be confused with an outspoken leader. The two are not simultaneous. An outspoken leader is usually a very opinionated person who just wants to be heard and validated. This is quite different from the leader who can be heard based on his team orientation.

"Leadership must be based on goodwill. Goodwill does not mean posturing and, least of all, pandering to the mob. It means obvious and wholehearted commitment to helping followers. We are tired of leaders we fear, tired of leaders we love, and tired of leaders who let us take liberties with them. What we need for leaders are men of the heart who are so helpful that they, in effect, do away with the need of their jobs. But leaders like that are never out of a job, never out of followers. Strange as it sounds, great leaders gain authority by giving it away." Admiral James B. Stockdale.

This is the next level to being an ExO leader. If you have grasped who you are as a leader, then it's time to give that authority away. It's not time to get comfortable so you can climb the ladder of popularity. A leader has a responsibility to empower others. Instead of stockpiling authority, a healthy leader gives that authority away in order to see other leaders learn, mature and grow into a healthy leader. The problem lies in the hunger for power. When a leader reaches a certain pinnacle, he tends to hoard that power. That pinnacle is reached when he has a large amount of control, either designated or given through healthy means. *The issue is not about power, but about what a leader does with it.* Powerful leaders are influential people. They can either use it to help feed a hunger for power, or they can lighten their "power load" and give some of it away by empowering others and teaching them how to lead in a healthy way. This keeps the checks and balances in account. This is not only healthy for a powerful leader, but it benefits those around him who need to be mentored and raised up, being taught how to be a healthy leader. They will in turn teach others.

In the world of finance, we see men and women who have fed the hungry beast of greed. Instead of denying themselves of this destructive behavior, they have moved towards it, using their positional power to manipulate finances, bonuses, taxes and the like. A web is woven through their network of people who help feed this beast and help keep the silence, all the while giving this leader more power, which he uses to influence others.

You see, it's not about authority, but about influence. Leaders influence people either towards health or into a power trip. Guiding someone to health means you, the leader, will mentor them that way. It's about having a desire to share with them those things that work. An arrogant leader will instead hoard what he knows and selfishly keep it for himself so he can continue to gain more and more power, distancing himself from the more "common" leaders. Arrogant, unhealthy leaders want to be the frontrunners. He will not allow himself to be burdened or bogged down with those who are less than he is. If he does, he is forced to give away his secret to success, which also means he is giving away power, leaving him with less control. To an unhealthy leader, dominance of power means the ability to control people, giving him the upper hand in the company. He oftentimes creates a path full of lies and deception, which he would have to guard and protect. This means he would have no other choice but to distance himself from others so his lies and deception cannot be found out. Mentoring is not in his vocabulary.

A healthy leader looks at mentoring others as an opportunity. They don't hoard what they know, but willingly and freely give it to others for their benefit. In all reality, it will benefit the company and the team will become stronger as people are not competing for position in order to become the top dog. The health of the organization is visible. Those who work there are not worried about the ladder, but are more concerned with the strength of those on the ladder.

Do you believe that? Are you that kind of leader? My hope is that through these few pages, you've been able to learn, evaluate and make some new personal and professional goals. This is not a book about becoming the perfect leader. Instead, it's about you, as a leader, leading in the healthiest way possible. This is going to be your decision. This is your journey - capitalize on it! Make the most of it! And last, but not least, take a long look into the mirror and accept what you see – the good (because you have some), the bad (yes, that's in there too), and the untapped potential that is waiting to be revealed. There's no better time than now to begin to change and become an extraordinary leader.

Another key to being an ExO leader is *communication*. As a leader, you already have a voice. But just because you have a voice does not mean people will listen to you. What makes you listen to someone who has a title attached to his name? Sometimes it's by the very nature of his title. For instance, the President of our nation, or someone in a high level capacity of our government. Maybe it's because he is successful and has been instrumental in making a difference in one way or another. It's possible you've read a book by a particular author and it's changed your life, so you give ear to them and can't wait for their next book. But what if you worked for the President, or someone on his team and you were mistreated? What if you met that prestigious author and he was arrogant and barked at his personal assistant with ridiculous demands? How would that change your view of him? Would you continue to read his material? Would you still support your government? I'm referring to communicating with respect. Everyone is a communicator, but not everyone communicates in a positive way.

As a team leader, you need to work at your communication skills. It may sound clear to you, but does it sound clear to others? The only way to find out is by asking them. "Am I being clear?" or, "Do you understand what I'm asking you to do?" If they have a blank stare or a delayed response, keep going until they understand what you are saying. This tells your staff that you are willing to change how you communicate in order for them to be committed to your team. Respecting them in this way will open doors of communication that are vital to a team's unity.

On that note, as you are communicating, are you motivating others? Stop and think about what you say and how you say it. Are the words you are choosing "up" words or are they "down" words? The language you use can either build people up or tear them down. Is your tone and language forceful or motivating? For example: let's say you see that one of your staff members could really use some encouragement in the area of time management. Stop right here and take a second to think about how you would handle that and what you would say. How would you *approach* them? Where would you have this meeting? What *tone* of voice would you use? What *strategic words* would you choose to get your point across?

Let's begin with **approach**. People know when something is wrong. If that is the case, there is going to be mystery overshadowing your meeting. Work at eliminating as much mystery as possible. Unhealthy leaders love the mystery because mystery means power: "I know something you don't know." Mystery is used as leverage and feeds a power hungry leader. An ExO leader would be willing to say to this staff member, *"Excuse me. I would like to visit with you this afternoon for just a couple of minutes. I've got some things I'd like to run by you. Would 2 o'clock work well for you?"* Notice the first line and the last line: both of them are respectful and not forceful. If they agree to that, suggest a non-threatening place. If it's your office, I suggest you don't sit behind your desk with a note pad in front of you. There are many lines on that pad, and if you write small there could be many, many issues confirming their fear of what you're about to say. So let me suggest that you either come out from behind your desk or sit across from them in a chair without the note pad on your lap, or meet at a non-threatening place such as a coffee establishment. The point is this: let them envision this meeting with little uncertainty.

The next thing is the **tone**. The second line uses the words, "I would like…". A leader has the option to say, "Hey, I've got to meet with you today. Come to my office at 2:00." It's forceful and demanding, leaving no room for respect. If a staff member comes to this meeting fearful, he isn't going to hear you. Be thoughtful of your tone and what condition you want this team member to be in when he comes to your meeting.

Also pick **strategic words**. On the third line, notice it says, "I've got some things I'd like to *run by you.*" If you use strategic words like, "talk to you about," or "things I have to discuss with you," you've left them with the feeling, "Uh oh. I'm in trouble." If you are already leading your team in a healthy way, they will have a relationship with you and determine they aren't in trouble and if there is an issue, you will gently walk them through it with health and restoration in mind.

Last is **respect.** "Would 2 o'clock work well for you?" is sending the message that you are willing to work with their schedule, and choosing not to be demanding. Everyone in your office knows that you have the power and position to go to anyone on your staff and demand they meet you when and where you tell them to. Might I suggest that is not the healthy way to lead? Respect goes a long way. But for the unhealthy leader, it's difficult to respect staff members because it feels as though he is giving his power away. In reality, respect is the most powerful thing a leader can give. Without it you won't be heard or respected by others, and your position will represent a place of fear in the minds of your staff members. Be willing to respect and work with their schedule. They may have some time dated things that you don't know about. Give them the option to either agree to that time, or suggest an alternative time. Be workable and always be respectful!

These suggestions are simply that: suggestions for you to begin thinking like a healthy, ExO leader so you can adjust your leadership style. Pick apart what you already do so you can see the good and strengthen the weak that you need to make stronger areas. Evaluating is a must. You need to self-evaluate your leadership style, but you also need to have others evaluate your style as well.

Allowing them to be a part of the change speaks volumes.

How I got here

You may be wondering why I was inspired to write this book. After all, I've not been in the top echelon of a major company, nor have I been the president of an organization. The experience I do have is one of pain. I have been through the trauma of being under unhealthy leadership. I have gone through the stages of post-traumatic stress disorder because of the trauma. I have come out on the other side much more alert to healthy and unhealthy when it comes to leadership. I am now much more aware of how leaders around me lead, including how I lead. You see, when you've been through the ongoing effects of an unhealthy leader, it forever changes the way you see leaders and hopefully the way you lead. Beyond that, it has helped me be a better person, including a better mom, wife, friend, etc. This is not just an on-the-job change. Rather, it's a life change to work towards health in your leadership style.

There is a belief that suggests when hurt by someone you ought to move closer to him. This is false. This is a common belief in those who abuse. In order for him to deal with his guilt, he wants, and even demands you move closer to him so they can feel better about what he's done and to feel like you are not turning your back on him in rejection. When someone is hurt, there needs to be a span of time where they go to a safe place and heal. If this does not happen and the offender continues to offend, then the mind, emotions and body begin to build a wall of protection from the continuing injury, much like an insulator. As long as that insulator, (which is a gift to the body to protect it), shields the mind, body and emotions from the on-going trauma, it seems as though everything will be okay. But there are a few stages that will arise from this event. Here are the stages I went through.

The first stage of my trauma lasted about a month. I would sit and blankly stare at the wall of my bedroom having day mares. I felt as though I had been in a traumatic car accident. I could "see" myself sitting alongside a busy highway, with debris from an accident strewn around and a burgundy SUV, which had rolled and was crashed, sitting in front of me. I "sat" on the curb on the side of the road wondering how I ended up outside of this vehicle, and by the looks of it I also wondered how I was still alive. I was numb and my emotions were unresponsive to the trauma. I was in shock. In order for my emotions to handle what was happening to me on a professional and occupational level, my psyche allowed me to experience the reality of what my situation was. I truly felt like I'd been in a traumatic car accident, but was all alone, without passengers to identify what I'd gone through. This is where the inner turmoil began.

The second stage was to find footing in the truth and walk that out. It is vital to find a trusted friend, or in some cases a counselor, who can help you reason what is reality, but also to help you understand why you feel the way you do and how to handle it. Finding the truth in a situation gives you footing and the ability to rise above the circumstances. If someone who is in a difficult situation does not find out the truth about what's happening, it's like a vortex that sucks them in while throwing them around and getting hit with debris. But if you stop and pull yourself out of the whirlwind of emotions and circumstances long enough to discover what's really going on, then the ability to find the truth is available to you. For example: if you are under an unhealthy, or even abusive leader, it is easy to feel guilty for how you're being treated. At this point one may feel like he deserves to be treated this way because he has failed his leader and the team, but only because this is the message that is being sent to him. If this is the case, examine what's *really* going on. The leader may be threatened by you and wants to replace you. It could also be they are making it hard on you to push you out of the organization.

What is the truth? Is it either of those things, or is it just time for this leader to do some inner changing? Is he feeling the pressure to do that but is resisting it, causing that resistance to flow out onto others? Are you really the problem? Are you in the wrong? Do you agree with this leader's vision? If you don't, you should consider finding a new place of work before you cause division within the team.

The third stage in my life was to rise above it and not let it ruin my life. That is easier said than done, since there is integrity involved. The things you do in this kind of moment must be well thought out, since you can let your immediate response temporarily allow you to feel better, but in the long run ruin your future because of a negative and equally unhealthy response. The complex part is in all the little things, such as causing division on the team, depending on the circumstances. My circumstances demanded that I keep it silent. The back draft of this decision is that without moral support from those on the team, you basically die, which I did. You die from your passion and eventually want nothing to do with the unhealthy leader, what they represent or anything that resembles their leadership. To rise above it don't dwell on it, but just endure until you can get to a new job. That takes time and patience. There may be residual physical effects during this period. Watch out for ulcers, heart palpitations, high blood pressure and migraines. Find places of peace and things to laugh about. Work through this very difficult stage. It's an uphill battle, but it will be worth it as you walk into your new job knowing you did it – you made it and you never have to go back. Don't have any strings attached. Do all you can to keep your integrity. An unhealthy leader can take a lot of things from you, but he can't take your integrity; you give that away yourself. Your integrity is one thing you can keep and take with you. It's worth it, so protect it!

The fourth stage is moving into a new and healthy job. Once under a healthy and safe leader, the body begins to let that intense guard down. It is at this point when the body, mind and emotions realize what happened.

This is when physical, emotional and psychological issues can appear. When the inner core of your being feels safe, it begins to come out of hiding. Unaware of this, you may find yourself to be more edgy, jumpy and irritable. This is the beginning of the end of your trauma. You may seem to be forgetful, confused or easily disillusioned. You may seem lethargic about life and somewhat depressed. These are warning signals to pay attention to and deal with. Don't ignore these things. One of the tips of the iceberg is chest pain. I experienced chest "congestion" for about a month. I researched heart diseases and every known issue with the heart until I found what matched my symptoms. I realized I had post traumatic stress disorder. Commonly, this name is attached to war veterans who've come back from war and haven't been able to deal with what they saw and experienced. In the midst of battle, you just pull up your bootstraps and get through it. This is exactly what I had to do. People who've been in traumatic events like car accidents, or criminal and abusive situations commonly experience this disorder. Psychologically I'd been through a traumatic roll over accident and eventually had to deal with it.

    I could not have gotten through my traumatic event without having faith in God. He alone gave me the peace and strength to pass through my "valley of the shadow of death" as it says in Psalm 23. When I went to a new job and was under a healthy, non-intimidating and safe leader, my guard slowly began to come down, without my telling it to. As that happened, there were emotions and feelings that had not been processed yet, due to the fact that the environment was not safe enough for me to let any wall come down. As physical things surfaced, I was able to track them and find the root of the issue and deal with it. I was able to truly let the trauma slowly go and realize I was now safe. Listen to your body and emotions and let them help you recover from your trauma. It won't last forever, but at some point, the last few strings will need to be cut for you to have a successful and healthy life and future.

    You see being an unhealthy leader is a negative thing. And being under one is one of the most painful things an employee can go through. Some leaders or their organizations have been sued because of emotional trauma. I am not suggesting one should do that or I would have done it myself. But unhealthy leaders should sit up and take notice of their decisions, as it will not only adversely affect those in their staff or work force, but it has the potential to ruin their reputation, credibility and potentially their organization. Much is at stake for an unhealthy leader. Eventually, word gets out. These things do not stay a secret forever. His reputation will supersede him and finding good help or staff members to hire will be very difficult.

Integrity: What's it worth to you?

The bottom line is this: Being an unhealthy leader isn't worth it. Having a leadership gifting can be one of the more rewarding gifts if used in the right way. Healthy leadership is a positive force that makes the world go around. It grows companies, people and it keeps innovation at it's best. There is no replacement for a healthy leader. An organization can have money growing on their money tree, but if there isn't a healthy leader to grow the people who pick the money off the tree, then you might as well cut the tree down and close the doors to your business. Employees and staff members enjoy working for healthy leaders. They feel safe. They dream big dreams. They produce more. It's a win, win situation.

Jesus teaches some things about integrity that we should take notice of. If you have done any study of Him, you may have noticed that the people Jesus used the strongest language with were the religious leaders. Why was Jesus so hard on them? It was because they were the teachers of God's law, but yet that law wasn't written on their hearts. They lived by the law, but didn't include love or grace.

Take for example Jesus' words to them in Matthew 23. He tells them they are frauds because they make sure every "i" is doted and every "t" crossed. But they lacked the basic values of love and grace. Integrity is not just about doing things the right way. Integrity is also how you treat others. It's very easy to make it all look good, but there's much more going on behind the scenes that won't stay hidden forever. Jesus, in this same chapter, went so far as to call these religious leaders "road blocks to God's kingdom." When I read a statement like that, I stop to ask myself if that is what I am. Am I a roadblock to what God wants to do in others lives? Religious pride steals integrity quickly because it says your opinion is the same as God's. Who is going to stand up against that? With that as a premise of making decisions, then integrity takes a back burner. This type of leading has climbed the one-leader ladder, leaving no room for accountability.

When a leader begins his solo trek upward, one rung at a time, the rules get more rigid for others, but not for him. The higher he gets, the less integrity he has, because honesty won't get him to the top of the world. This causes him to implement strict rules on others, including a lot of demands, in order for him to have what he deems as an open policy for himself. This is where integrity gets pushed aside and wrong, even illegal dealings are begun. This type of leading has landed many leaders in jail. Before you judge them, remember that you have the same potential. The only way to combat a lack of integrity is to pursue things that are integral. Because we are all born sinful, and battle our sinful nature throughout our lifetimes, it is vital that we seek out behavior that is upright and untainted. A lack of integrity is poisonous. It poisons the leader, his family, and the organization.

In The Light

In order for your dark side, the side that craves to be in control and to control others, to be shut out purpose to do all your dealings in the light. Simply put, this means to not do your dealings in the dark. I am not speaking of nighttime. I am referring to secretly dealing with particular people whom you know do not deal with integrity. If you cannot share your dealings openly with your staff or your board members, then you need to stop the shady process and get into the light. Leaders who deal in the dark do so to reach their goal by manipulating and cohersing others. This takes some creative dealings. The disappointing part about this type of leading is that he has a staff and board members who are relying on his leadership. If his leadership is causing them to be blinded to the truth, then he is like a wolf leading the lambs to slaughter. At some point, he will be caught and as he falls from his ladder of exultation, those rungs in the ladder won't feel as powerful as they did while climbing them. Oh, they will have a powerful punch mind you. But going down is not only painful, but humiliating.

Leading in the light is choosing to live above board. This type of leading allows the team to function with freedom and not suspicion. A healthy leader seeks out light oriented avenues. His life and dealings are open and honest. He has nothing to hide. That is powerful. What some leaders think is power will only cause them to fall. But leading with integrity and in the light is a power that is spread to everyone on the team. It allows <u>for</u> the team to be successful, which inadvertently brings success to the main leader. That is a healthy ExO leader.

Measuring Success

What one leader deems success, another may not. You cannot base your success on anything other than your goals, and how they are met. It takes a leader who embraces value to bring success to his team. So the question is: What is success to you and what is success to your team? If you and your team embrace different values of what success is, disappointment will flourish. Is it how many people in your community find salvation? Could it be how many new members you receive into your congregation? Maybe success to you is just getting a day off! Does your team measure success by the amount in the offering, the number of visitors to your church, or the cutting edge, culturally relevant music? Remember: you can't please everyone. Whatever the opinions are, success is just around the corner. Success comes everyday through something we call "opportunity." Every leader has the choice to be successful. If he passes by the opportunities he may fail.

To measure success, ask the people around you how you're doing. A simple survey or evaluation is beneficial and I encourage you to use specific ones on a regular basis. When I see a successful person, based on what I feel success is, I want to meet his family. What condition are they in? A leader may have three homes, speak around the world, or have 12 CD's and 5 of them gold platinum. But if his family is not in good shape, then I do not view this leader as successful, no matter what his name is or how many books he's written. Success to me is when a leader has strong personal character, not just strong skill in his calling.

There are **five qualities a church leader should have** based on Titus 1:5-9, adapted from The John Maxwell Leadership Bible:

1. Personal life: blameless, not self-willed, not quick-tempered, not violent, sober-minded, holy, self-controlled.
2. Family life: husband of one wife, with faithful children.
3. Social life: hospitable, not accused of dissipation, not given to wine.
4. Financial life: a steward of God, not greedy for money.
5. Professional life: not accused of insubordination, a love of what is good, just, holding fast to faithful word, able to exhort and convict those who contradict.

That's a good road map for success. To be successful takes preparation and perseverance. Success doesn't just happen. It takes living life in such a way that God is lifted above everything else. This allows the four above points to be worked into all areas of life. Prepare to be successful by how you parent your children, how you love your wife, and how you treat your staff. Persevere through the tough times when team action is bottle necked and everyone is trying to squeeze their idea of success through.

As a Christian, success to me is when a life has been touched, changed or transformed by truth, love and forgiveness. My goal as a leader is to point people to Jesus through my words, actions and behaviors. I cannot be all things to all people. But what I can do is be an example of healthy leadership. The first thing I can example is humility, then love and grace. That is part of how I view success.

I also see success as being able to accurately communicate ones vision to a team and bring them to a place of agreement and then move forward. I do believe that the end results are important and that the goals in a vision should be met, but the people meeting the goals with me are more important. If I can lead a team with health, that means with humility, servanthood, trust and confidence, then the end results should be as we projected and worked for. If we don't meet the goal the way we wanted to, the team should not dismantle because of it. If I have communicated my vision, given my team a voice, and we've made forward motion with unity, then I see that as successful. The results of those components are: met goals and vision fulfilled. Leading in this way is not only healthy and extraordinary, but a whole lot of fun! Of course there is no such thing as a perfect leader, team or plan. But when healthy leaders do their part, the world is a better place one organization at a time.

Why Do I Do This?

Do you enjoy leading? Why do you like to lead? Go back to the basics for a moment. Have you thought about what makes leading fun? That answer will change with each leader, but one common thread is that you like to watch and participate in the leaders around you changing and maturing in their leadership abilities.

So what does it take to be not only a good leader, but a healthy one? Faithfulness. It takes your being willing to stay tied to your post and be in it for the long haul. It takes faithfulness on your part to see others through their stages of learning. It's exhausting but if you can stay faithful to your staff, and to the vision, good things will happen.

It also takes openness to be a good leader. Share what you know. Don't make up things you know nothing about, just to make yourself higher than you really are. Just share your dreams, visions and your life. Pass on your gift through mentoring. Take time to pour into a life. You won't regret it.

So how about you? Are you a healthy leader? Healthy leaders are leaders who are willing to change. They are not intimidating, demanding or forceful. Are you willing to look at how you currently lead, including asking those around you to evaluate your leadership? What kind of leader do you want to be? You create that person through your choices. There's no better time than now to choose to begin changing. It's a process. It's going to take time. But chances are, those around you are going to be willing to walk that journey with you. Let them in on your choice. Welcome to the world of healthy leaders.

"You cannot be a leader, and ask other people to follow you, unless you know how to follow, too."

Sam Rayburn

ExO 7
Focus

To end our time together, I felt it was fitting to leave you with some focus about what an ExO leader is. Focus is described as the center of interest. To be an ExO leader, it is going to take some focus and maybe some realignment of your vision to become who you desire to be. In this case, there are five things I would like to leave you centered on that should help you keep your **F.O.C.U.S.**

F – *reedom*
ExO leaders not only live in freedom in their own lives, but they help other leaders know how to do that also. Freedom as a leader is being secure and confident in how you lead. If you are unstable and lack confidence, you cannot lead a team to success. Freedom brings all team members to a level playing field around the table. It allows them the availability to express their dreams with certainty that they will be heard and validated. Freedom is powerful. Being free to dream, even free to fail in this safe environment, produces a healthy team.

O – *pportunity*

There are many opportunities to be an ExO leader. From the morning cup of coffee to the evening news, your day is filled with moments where you can touch a life. When I volunteer to return the shopping cart for an elderly couple, they have no idea who I am, my title or that I have authored a book. Look for opportunities to be an extraordinary person. Out of that, you will have no trouble being an ExO leader. ExO leaders are also extraordinary fathers, mothers, wives, husbands, sons, daughters, and citizens. Seize the opportunities you have daily to be extraordinary in everyday life, and let that spill over into your profession.

C – *ommitment*
In order to be an ExO leader, it takes commitment to a cause. That cause is to further God's kingdom through your example of healthy leadership. Through healthy leadership, you will assist those who have been wounded by unhealthy leaders by restoring their trust in leadership. That alone takes deep commitment as wounded people wound others and need patience and grace shown to them. Stay committed to change. That might not seem right, but allow me to explain. Stability is a staple in the life of a leader. Change is not unstable, but is necessary to lead with freedom and seize opportunities. Commitment to change is vital to a team and to your being an ExO leader.

U – *nity*
This may not seem possible, depending on the circumstances you find yourself in. You may have inherited a disheveled team. The first order of business to instilling unity on your team is to give them a vision based on where you see the organization going. Those goals are things like integrity, open dialogue, team involvement, and

trust. Those are basic principles that will remain with you at the helm and hopefully well beyond. These principles, along with others, will spread beyond your team and will influence an entire organization. Unity can be achieved. It is not out of reach. When you give your team a purpose, mixed with attainable goals, unity will happen. If there are team members who do not belong on your team, you will need to consider moving them into a team where they do belong. Unity is vital and it is attainable.

S – *ervant*
Enough cannot be said about servant leadership. When a leader brings his team together and uses the opportunity to serve them and show them how to serve others, a desired comradery will begin. Servant leadership is a team's biggest strength. Without it, they will bicker and eventually implode. You cannot have a solid team without service as a key component. Serving others is actually fun. What has someone done for you recently, as an act of service that touched your life? It doesn't have to be major things, such as cashing in all your savings bonds and giving it away. It can be as simple as bringing extra bagels to the office one morning, or maybe taking the entire office to coffee. The little things are usually the most impacting because it's possible to continue doing little things often, rather than big things once a year. With all the responsibilities on a leader's plate, how often does he stop long enough to think of serving someone else? Not often, which is what makes the healthy leader extraordinary!

    After writing this last section of my book, I came upon an amazing, real life story about an ExO leader that I must share with you. I was amazed and pleased, as this leader seems to use many of the principles I've described for you throughout my book. There are a few things I would like you to notice. The article is by Caroline Louise Cole, written for BNET.com, an online management advice website. The title of her article is, <u>Eight Values Bring Unity to a Worldwide Company</u>, written in March 2001.

The story is about a company named General Semiconductor. They are a major supplier of tiny transistors, diodes, and rectifiers that control the electronic impulses that power everything from automobiles and cell phones to dishwashers and personal computers. General Semiconductor turns out over 17 million of these minute parts a day, each wholesaling for well under a dollar. Customers include all the major electronics manufacturers, among them Phillips, Sony, and Delta. When Ronald Ostertag became the head of this company, he discovered some inner turmoil between a few of the core staff. In fact, it came to a head between two of the men as they began to bicker before a presentation in front of the board of directors. Ostertag said, "It was then I realized that not only were people at the very top of the company going in different directions, they were not listening to each other or respecting what others had to say."

    Ostertag did what he had to do. He replaced nearly every member of his senior team. "But that quickly manifested itself in job insecurity further down the ranks, and I realized we needed to do something to develop a sense of teamwork," he says. "We needed a mission statement and we needed to develop a culture of mutual respect that fostered cooperation and innovation. Ostertag says he brought his new team together at a brainstorming session to come up with the company's core principles... From around the table came words like "quality" and "integrity" and phrases like "good customer service" and "on-time delivery."

Notice: Ostertag recognized disunity, made some initial decisions to bring cohesion and followed that through by allowing the new team to bring their voices and dreams to the table. He wanted to hear what they had to say. He validated their voices and they produced the eight values that this company, years later, still function with. They believe so deeply in those values that they had them printed on their company credit cards. At any given moment, Ostertag would ask his employees what five of those key values were. He wanted to know if his employees were living out the fundamental values of this company.

Cole continued the story by writing, "The company instituted a program called People Plus that involves a conventional 360-degree review of each employee using a comprehensive self-assessment matched with feedback from supervisors, managers, peers, and subordinates chosen by the employee. But it includes a twist. Once the written evaluations are completed, each staffer, from Ostertag down, meets privately with an outside psychologist to discuss what the reports said and what behavioral adjustments the staffer might consider. "We're quite serious when we talk about leadership even to a bench worker on the assembly line," says Gary Barello, a human resources staffer. "Lots of people will say, 'Oh, I'm not a leader,' but when we point out that the essence of leadership is influence, they realize everyone has leadership qualities and responsibilities."

Notice: Ostertag, the man at the helm, allowed

himself to be evaluated! He wants his company to stay focused – F.O.C.U.S. He recognizes that anyone has the potential to be a leader by just being influential. Everyone in this company matters and they obviously work hard at making sure they know that. That takes a non-threatened servants heart to accomplish. Ostertag and his team seek out the "talents and contributions" of those in every aspect of their company. Everyone matters.

Ostertag continues by saying, "I really believe that empowering employees is the key to any company's success, but you can't do that unless everyone is working from the same knowledge base." So he set his human resources staff to the task of finding out what employees wanted to know about the company."

Notice: This company functions in the light – out in the open because their leader does. He understands that if you want people to work their best and commit to your vision, they need to be able to ask the big questions. This allows them to have ownership in a healthy way. It also keeps the leader from owning it all and becoming territorial. This is an extraordinary way to live.

And finally, Cole finished the interview with Ostertag and a few of his staff members. "No question was off-base; we took everyone seriously," says Barello, the human resource project's manager. Once he had the questions in hand, he then assembled a group of "subject matter experts" to answer them. What human resources eventually produced was a 135-page standard three-ring binder of information that includes everything from a list of the company's board of directors and history to a description of products, customers, and competitors to basic finances. Ostertag credits the attention to staff interaction and cooperation with helping the company to nearly double revenues since 1996 and achieve greater market share. "From our perspective in human resources, these programs have translated into a very stable workforce with little turnover, whether we are talking about our manufacturing plant in Ireland or in Europe," Perry says. The average length of service among the six-member human resources team is 13 and a half years. For the technical marketing support group, staff longevity is about 12 years, 9 months.

This is just remarkable. This company gets it. They see that the success lies within the horizontal way of leading. Imagine what would happen to this company if Ostertag would lead the vertical way. It wouldn't take long and the staff and employees would feel devalued and would lose their passion. They would essentially be sidelined. Ostertag and the human resources manager understand that if you keep the doors open, giving everyone a voice and an avenue into the heart of the company, then longevity will most certainly be sustained. They have proven the basic principles of ExO leading to be true. Whether you are a CEO or a pastor, these principles will work. Let your staff be a part of the vision you have. Don't keep your cards so close to your chest. You have an incredible team just waiting to take your vision and multiply it. Give it, share it and pass it on! Leadership is an inspiring position to have. As you have read, you don't need a title to be a leader, just a person of influence. So whether you have a title or not, work towards not only being influential but also extraordinary. There's a world waiting for the potential you have to pour out and there's a team waiting to change the world with you!

Questionnaire

Personal Evaluation:
What kind of leader are you?

What are you doing that is working and is healthy?

What do you need to change about your leadership style?

What kinds of people have been entrusted to you? Review them by their talents. Validate them today, and tomorrow, and the next day, and every day after that. Write down some names and the things you see.

If someone were to write the story of your leadership, what would it say? Ask someone under your leadership to do that, if you're brave enough.

About The Author

Robin Liebe, a Montana native, has been in a position of leadership since 1994. She, along with her husband Dan, have worked with teenagers through the local church through training and mentoring, and are currently Montana District Youth Directors in the Assemblies of God with the job of overseeing the children's, youth and college age ministries. Robin has also been a part of training leadership teams, mobilizing them to lead teenagers through the stages of their lives. She has also drawn from many personal experiences through healthy and unhealthy leadership styles by being involved in various staff settings within and outside of the church.

  Robin has a strong desire to see leaders function in their sphere of influence, rather than through their power. She believes it takes more than a title to be a leader as it encompasses relationship as well. In order to be an extraordinary leader, Robin believes one must function out of humility and lead with a servant mentality. This combination is what she has written about and believes it will revolutionize leadership, evolving from an ordinary leader to an extraordinary one.